D0189084

Hiking in Israel

First Edition 2008

The Toby Press LLC

A Paperback Original

POB 8531, New Milford, CT 06776-8531, USA
& POB 2455, London W1A 6YW, England
& POB 4044, Jerusalem 91040, Israel

www.tobypress.com

Co Authors: Ya'acov Shkolnik and Yadin Roman
Photographers: Ya'acov Shkolnik, Yadin Roman, Doron Horowitz, Efrat Nakash, Tagist Ron.
Cover photo: Efrat Nakash
Translators and Editors: Judy Davidson and Heidi J. Gleit
Art Director: Limor Tabeka
Designer: Sonia Pundik
Cover Designer: Tani Bayer, The Toby Press

ISBN 978 1 59264 237 3

Printed and bound in Israel

HIKING IN ISRAEL
36 of Israel's Best Hiking Routes

BY THE EDITORS OF ERETZ MAGAZINE

Contents

Contents

Map of Israel

Introduction

With 10,000 kilometers of marked hiking trails, Israel is one of world's best-kept hiking secrets. Israel's varied landscapes, which range from the lush Mediterranean vegetation of the mountains of Galilee to the coastal plain and the local deserts that are part of the world desert belt, offer the hiker a myriad of different hiking experiences within a short distance of one another

Trail marking has been going on in Israel for over 50 years and there are excellent 1:50,000-scale trail maps of Israel's color-coded trails. For numerous reasons, ranging from the xenophobic to the pecuniary, the trail maps are published only in Hebrew. The largest scale map available in English is a series of 1:100,000-scale topographic maps, which do not have the trails on them.

For the last 20 years, ERETZ Magazine has been writing about the hiking trails of Israel – new trails, renewed trails, exciting routes, and more. In this book, we present 36 of what we think are the most exciting trails in Israel.

The trails are for hikers – people who have experience hiking and want to experience Israel in a different way. Before setting out on your hike, please carefully read the following guidelines for hiking in Israel and how to use this book and its maps. Hiking is a great pastime, but, like any other outdoor activity, it has its rules. Being careless in the great outdoors is dangerous

Finally, before we delve into the details, please help preserve the environment. Do not litter – carry your garbage with you and if you see other garbage on the way,

pick it up and take it with you also. Stick to the trails and take only pictures.

The Israeli Trail System

Israeli hiking trails are marked with a colored stripe, which is blue, green, red, or black, between two white strips. Paths to sites just off the trail are marked with a "clear" stripe – two white strips with no color between them.

At the beginning of a trail and at its end, or at trail junctions, the trail markings can appear in one of four different forms: on a sign stating the destination of the trail; on a sign of one of the various nature or regional organizations; on a road sign opposite the entrance to the trail; or on a stone or a little tin marker.

Along the trail, the markings will appear on rocks, metal pegs, tin signs, etc. The markings are in both directions and are close to each other. The trails usually are referred to by the color of their markers – "the green trail," "the red trail," etc.

Instructions for Hikers

Before setting out on your hike, call one of the trail coordination centers for advice about the trail, information about any last-minute changes, etc. Hikes on trails that go through military firing zones must be coordinated in advance at the coordination centers. Firing zones are usually, but not always, open to the public on weekends and holidays and therefore all hikes through them absolutely must be coordinated in advance.

To coordinate a hike or obtain advice,

call: Northern Coordination Center, (04) 676-5713; Haifa, (04) 867 5804; Tel Aviv, (03) 681-1152/3; Jerusalem, (02) 623-2811; South, (08) 627-9258.

Safety Guidelines

Hike only along marked trails.

Do not roll stones down slopes or mountains.

Do not insert your hand under stones or other objects – snakes and small animals tend to hide there to escape the summer or daylight heat.

Always bring first-aid equipment with you.

As a rule, drinking water is not available on the trails. Bring sufficient water with you.

Do not drink water from agricultural pipes – the water could contain fertilizer.

Drinking water allowance: in winter, three liters per person per day; and in summer, one liter per person per hour!

Hats and sunglasses are a must in Israel during both summer and winter.

Beware of flash floods. Do not enter riverbeds in desert areas when there is a flash flood warning on the radio. In any case, never enter desert riverbeds on stormy or rainy days.

Do not set out on a trail without the appropriate hiking map.

Using the Maps

The maps are in Hebrew. That said, the hiking trails on the maps are color coded and numbered. In the map diagrams in this book, we have stated the map needed for each hike, the color of the trail, and the number of the trail. Comparing our diagram of the hike to the map should help you obtain a good understanding of the

area through which the trail runs. The words might be in Hebrew, but the topography and markings are international.

For your convenience, there is a translation of the legend of the trail maps on the following pages.

A Few Final Words of Advice

Trails, roads, and even riverbeds can change. A map is only as accurate as the day it was drawn. Before setting out, get last-minute advice on the conditions in the field from the coordination centers, from the Israel Nature and Parks Authority, or from the field schools of the Society for the Protection of Nature in Israel.

Always let someone know where you are going and when you are expected back. If you can, take a cell phone with you.

Don't hike at night. If night falls, stay where you are and wait for daylight. It might be cold, but you won't get lost and you won't fall down a cliff.

Pay attention to the recommended months of the year for each hike (see page 16 for an explanation of the "Hiking Months Legend"). Hiking in the desert in summer is dangerous, so heed our instructions. Always wear hiking shoes. Sandals are not appropriate for hiking.

In general, wildlife in Israel is not dangerous. The few leopards in the desert or the wild boars in the north will keep out of your way. There are a few poisonous snakes, but they will not attack you (and if you are wearing shoes they won't be able to bite you). Be suspicious of wild animals that are not afraid of people. They could have rabies – keep away from them. And finally, most important of all, have fun!

Railway . . . .

Main Road . . . .

Regional Road . . . . . .

Local Road . . . .

Unpaved Road . . . . . .

Tracks and Trails . . . . .

Contours . . . .

Cliff . . . .

Canyon . . . .

Spot Height . . . .

Built-Up Area . . . . . .

Power Line . . . .

Building, Ruin . . . .

Ruins . . . .

Synagogue . . . .

Church . . . .

Mosque, Moslem Tomb . . . .

Tree, Wood . . . .

Cave . . . .

Antenna . . . .

Pumping Station . . . .

Quarry . . . .

Route Numbers

Distance in Km . . . . .

Kilometer Markers . . .

Nahal, Wadi . . . .

Canal, Aqueduct . . . . .

Spring, Well . . . .

Pool, Pond . . . .

Cistern . . . .

Fruit Trees . . . .

Citrus Trees . . . .

Olives . . . .

Vineyard . . . .

Natural Wood . . . .

Barren Land . . . .

Riverbed . . . .

Sand Dunes . . . .

Swamp . . . .

Maps: Selected Symbols of the Hiking and Trail Maps

All Vehicle Track . . . .

4X4 Track . . . .

Hiking Path . . . .

Short Hike . . . .

Jeep, Bike Route . . . .

Israel Trail . . . .

Israel Trail Information Booth . . . . . .

Hiking Path Number . . . .

Path . . . .

Nature Site . . . .

Park Boundary . . . .

Museum . . . .

Nature Park . . . .

Ancient Synagogue . . . .

JNF Site . . . .

Ancient Church . . . .

Park Name . . . . שְׁמוּרַת יָטְבָתָה.

Proposed Park . . . . . . שְׁמוּרַת אֲלִימוֹנִים.

Historical Site . . . .

War of Independence Site . . . .

Settlement Site . . . .

Viewpoint . . . .

Field School . . . .

Youth Hostel . . . .

Gas Station . . . .

Bathing Beach . . . .

Visitors' Center . . . .

Picnic Site . . . .

Camping Grounds . . . .

Camp Site . . . .

Hospital, Police, Ambulance . . . .

Firing Zone . . . .

International Border . . . . . .

When to Hike Legend

jan	feb	mar	apr	may	jun	jul	aug	sep	oct	nov	dec

Best months to hike . . . . | jan |

Hiking possible . . . . | mar |

Do not hike . . . . | apr |

Route 01:

Mighty Oaks and Waterfalls

A route for good hikers on the slopes of Mt. Hermon, from the Nebi Hazori oak grove to the Banias Spring, and along the Hermon River to Moshav She'ar Yashuv.

Route length: 12 km.
Difficulty: Good hikers. A relatively relaxed hike, on an incline.
Start point: Sayeret Egoz monument.
Access: From the Banias-Hermon road.
End point: Moshav She'ar Yashuv.
Duration: 8 hours, including a visit to Nimrod's Fortress National Park and sites in the Nahal Hermon Nature Reserve.
Admission fees: Admission charge to the national park and the nature reserve.
Opening hours:
National parks and nature reserves are open:
April to Sept.: 8 a.m. - 5 p.m.,
Fri. and holiday eves until 4 p.m.
Oct. to Mar.: 8 a.m. - 4 p.m.,
Fri. and holiday eves until 3 p.m.
Equipment: Regular.
Remarks: Locked gate on trail from Banias Waterfall to She'ar Yashuv: Ask a ranger to open it. If you wish to arrange this in advance, phone (04) 695-0272.
Pickup point for cars: She'ar Yashuv bridge. Buses should wait for hikers at the edge of the moshav.
Map: Golan and Hermon Hiking and Trail Map (No. 1).

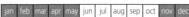

| jan | feb | mar | apr | may | jun | jul | aug | sep | oct | nov | dec |

Midway along the road leading up from Banias to Majdal e-Shams, beside the grave of Nebi Hazori, is a grove of large Kermes oak trees with unusual shapes. One of the trees, for example, has a hollow trunk, which someone has gone to the trouble of bolstering with stones. Another has a bowed trunk, but still affords a great deal of shade. But most important, between the trees you can see Mt. Hermon, its slopes covered with a dense grove of Kermes oaks that is the "ancestral homeland" of the trees of Nebi Hazori.

Some botanists say that in their natural form, Kermes oaks are only shrubs. Others maintain that in the right conditions, they would grow and flourish like the oaks of Nebi Hazori – which have certainly been given special treatment, due to the site's holiness for the local Druze population.

Sheikh Othman el-Hazori was a Druze holy man who was known as an ardent seeker of peace. Legend has it that the sheikh would present people passing through the area with a special kind of salt: it tasted good to peace lovers, but made warmongers so confused that they forgot their target.

The Jewish National Fund has installed a pleasant picnic site in the shade of the grove. Don't be alarmed by the fence surrounding the site: All you have to do is open the green gate and go in. If you prefer, you can stop at the little picnic site that is a bit further along, on the dirt road that is marked in red. This is the beginning of a relatively new marked trail which leads to Nimrod's Fortress.

A narrow path branches off from the red trail and leads to the Sayeret Egoz memorial for the fallen. Sayeret Egoz was an Israeli Special Forces unit that operated in this area in the 1970s. The monument is striking in its simplicity: in the shade of the limestone rocks characteristic of Mt. Hermon, small basalt stones bear the names of the fallen soldiers.

The dirt road leads up to a large plaza beside a grove of olive trees with impressive trunks. One trunk looks as twisted as a floor mop that has just been squeezed out. From the olive grove you can already see the eastern part of Nimrod's Fortress, a mountain spur further down the slope.

The trail leads through the grove, exiting beside another grove of ancient olive trees growing among the wild trees. At the edge of the olive grove, the red trail meets up with a blue trail, which ascends from the depths of the riverbed of Nahal Hazor. Now you are opposite the fence of the fortress. Follow the sign with the arrow pointing left and you will soon reach the main road, and the gate of Nimrod's Fortress National Park. Take one of the leaflets at the gate.

Nimrod's Fortress

Nimrod's Fortress was built by Almalek Alaziz Othman, the Ayyubid governor of Banias, in 1228. Later, when Baybars became the Mameluke sultan, he presented Nimrod's Fortress as a gift to Bilik, his loyal friend and second in-command. Historical sources relate that Bilik built several towers, a mosque, and a palace in the fortress. After Baybars's death, his son arranged for Bilik to be murdered, apparently because he feared his power.

With the murder of Bilik, construction work in the fortress ceased. Not only was it no longer needed, since the fortress was already large and strong enough, but its strategic value declined after the Crusaders were expelled from the Holy Land in 1291. After the Ottoman Turks conquered the land in 1517, they used the fortress as a luxury prison for Ottoman nobles who had been exiled to Palestine. The fortress was abandoned later in the sixteenth century.

The right way to visit Nimrod's Fortress is not to continue up the road, as the vehicles do. Instead, immediately after going through the gate, cross the little olive grove that is on the right and you'll come to a sign warning that this route should be attempted only by experienced hikers accompanied by an authorized guide acquainted with the site. If you're used to hiking, don't be intimidated by the sign – you'll manage without any difficulty.

Continue on the trail, which is well marked with stones along the side, and make your way up the steep slope, on a stepped path with a clear route, until you are at the foot of the eastern tower of the fortress. In the northern part of the tower, you'll see a small opening, which you can get through by crawling.

Beyond the opening is a passageway built of large, well-chiseled stones, which leads straight to the donjon, which is also the highest part of the castle. The view is splendid: from here you can easily see the slopes of Mt. Hermon, the northern Golan, and the Hula Valley.

A stroll through the fortress takes about an hour and should end up on the western side, where you'll find a snack bar, rest rooms, and several tables under a thatched roof – an appropriate place for a break.

To the Sources of Nahal Hermon

At the edge of the parking lot, set out on the trail marked in green. This route is also relatively new and it helps you to negotiate your way down the rocky slope.

Climb up the low ledge near the parking lot and then continue down the green trail to the Banias Spring. The trail descends along the watershed line of a gentle slope, where you'll find a sparse olive grove, accompanied by a large number of spiny broom bushes.

The view is magnificent. The mountains of southern Lebanon, the Hula Valley, and the Naftali Mountains are with you all along the way. A green line of plane trees meanders through the valley, marking the banks of Nahal Hermon.

The trail leads to the observation terrace offering a lovely view of the Banias Spring from atop the cliff, above the temple of Pan. The gleaming white temple stands beside the grave of Nebi Hadar on the slope to the right. To your left, the old mosque of Banias village is clearly visible beside the ruins of the walls of the Crusader town.

From the observation terrace, the trail leads down through a forest of Mt. Tabor oaks and reaches the fence of the nature reserve. Walk to the left, along the fence, until you reach an abandoned house. Beside it is a little opening in the gate. You can enter, but first pay at the ticket booth and take the leaflet describing the routes in the reserve.

All of the information you need is in the leaflet. Your first stop should be the ruins of the temple of Pan, which have undergone impressive reconstruction work. Then continue along the riverbed.

Banias Spring.

To the Banias Waterfall

From here on, the route is replete with water – the water that flows through Nahal Hermon. Head for the Banias Waterfall. The trail crosses over to the right bank of the river via a wooden footbridge, and then crosses back to the left bank. This path runs under the arches of a Roman bridge. Note the true laurel tree on the western part of the bridge.

After passing the abandoned hydroelectric station, you'll come to a nicely reconstructed flour mill. At times you can enjoy a Druze pita baked on the spot by a local concessionaire.

Before setting out for the trail that leads to the Banias Waterfall, make a detour to the left to the site of the Roman-period city of Banias, large portions of which were uncovered in archaeological excavations. Allow about an hour for a scramble through the ruins.

Follow the trail to the waterfall along the left bank of the river. After a short walk, you will reach an observation terrace offering a magnificent view of the most impressive waterfall in Israel. You can replenish your own water supply at the tap beside the observation point.

After enjoying the view of the waterfall from above, continue down the path to a footbridge that will take you across the river to the right bank. After crossing the bridge, you will reach a trail junction. The trail to the right leads back up the river to the waterfall, a two-minute walk. The trail to the left, with black markings, leads down the river to Moshav She'ar Yashuv.

Banias Waterfall.

Down Nahal Hermon

First walk up the path to the waterfall for a refreshing spray of cold water from the waterfall. Then retrace your steps down the river bank in the direction of She'ar Yashuv. Don't be alarmed when you come upon a locked gate: just ask the the reserve ranger on duty to open it for you.

This trail may be the only one in Israel that features a walk of several kilometers alongside a flowing river. After crossing a layer of hard black basalt rock, the river flows into a black canyon that is about 3 meters wide, turning into a torrent of white water. You get to view the river from above, that is, from the high ledge that you're walking on.

At the end of the narrow canyon, follow the trail leading down to the river. It will take you to a beautiful, shady spot beside the water, where you'll find an overturned Syrian tank, half submerged in the river. During the Six Day War, five Syrian tanks tried to attack Kibbutz Dan, which is located about 2 kilometers to the west. The Syrian armored attack was beaten back by the Israeli Defense Forces. This particular tank miscalculated its retreat and ended up falling into the river. The tank's belly makes a good dining surface, but please don't leave any leftovers from your picnic behind afterwards.

Return to the trail and continue to walk along the ledge high above the river. When you come to a lovely cluster of large Mt. Tabor oaks, look at the opposite slope, on the eastern bank. Usually, you can see the waterfall of Nahal Pera, which descends

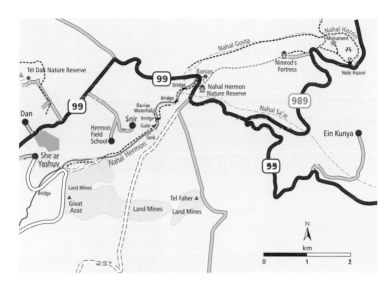

from the ruins of the village of Ein Fit and splashes into Nahal Hermon In a series of three steps with a total height of some 70 meters. In especially rainy years water continues to flow down the waterfall even in the height of summer.

The trail continues along the ledge on the western side of Nahal Hermon. After about 300 meters, the trail passes beneath large jujube trees. Above the trees, on the slope of the river bank, is a travertine step hewn with burial niches that date back to the Roman period.

The trail continues down the river and soon a line of large plane trees appear on the river banks. The trail crosses over to the left bank, where you will spot a dirt road (suitable for jeeps) that climbs up the left bank of the river and reaches an unpaved dirt road.

Instead of walking along this road, take the trail marked in red that branches off to the right. It continues along the river, between fig, willow, and plane trees and sometimes through a "reed tunnel."

When you see the three gigantic Mt Tabor oaks to the left of the trail, you'll know that you're nearly at the end of the route. This used to be the site of the tomb of Sheikh Mahafi, near a small spring that flows in a narrow rivulet to Nahal Hermon. Take a moment to enjoy the shade of the trees and marvel at their size.

Now all that remains to be done is to continue a bit further, meet up with the unpaved road, and follow it to the bridge that leads to She'ar Yashuv, the ending point of the hike.

Route 02:
Nahal Hazori

A beautiful Golan ravine leads to a Crusader bridge and continues with a descent into a narrow ravine, affording a magnificent view of Nimrod's Fortress.

Route length: 2 km.
Difficulty: Moderate.
Start point: Nebi Hazori.
Access: Route 889, between kilometer markers 5 and 6.
End point: Entrance to Nimrod's Fortress National Park.
Duration: 2-3 hours.
Admission fees: Admission charge to the national park and the nature reserve.
Opening hours:
National parks and nature reserves are open:
April to Sept.: 8 a.m. - 5 p.m.,
Fri. and holiday eves until 4 p.m.
Oct. to Mar.: 8 a.m. - 4 p.m.,
Fri. and holiday eves until 3 p.m
Equipment: Regular.
Remarks: After the rains, the stones along the river are very slippery.
Pickup point for cars: End of route.
Map: Golan and Hermon Hiking and Trail Map (No. 1).

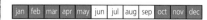

| jan | feb | mar | apr | may | jun | jul | aug | sep | oct | nov | dec |

From the picnic site adjacent to the grave of Nebi Hazori, descend into Nahal Hazori along a trail marked in blue. At the bottom of the meadow, where the trail reaches the riverbed, is an intact Crusader bridge. The bridge, that today seems to lead nowhere, was on the main road from Tyre to Damascus — one of the most important highways during the Middle Ages and the main reason for the construction of the huge Nimrod's Fortress. The trail follows the riverbed to the remains of two water mills.

Past the water mills, the trail meanders between large oak trees and shrubs to a point where the deep ravine of Nahal Hazori can be seen. In the autumn and winter the ground between the trees is covered with a colorful carpet of flowers.

From this point, the trail descends into the ravine of Nahal Hazori. The descent takes time and includes some strenuous stepping from one stone to the other and squeezing among huge boulders.

Near its end, the ravine turns sharply to the left, affording you a magnificent view of Nimrod's Fortress. Once out of the ravine, a

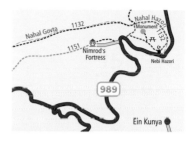

trail junction is reached. **Be careful not to miss it!** The blue trail turns left and returns to the road near the entrance to the Nimrod's Fortress National Park. Take this trail. The trail that continues along the riverbed, marked in black, goes to Nahal Govta and continues to the Banias Nature Reserve. The blue trail makes its way gently up the slope to an olive grove. Making its way through the grove, the trail reaches the entrance to the Nimrod's Fortress National Park.

Once at the entrance to the national park, the designated driver can jog from here uphill for 10-15 minutes to the place where the cars are parked.

Nimrod's Fortress.

Devora and Gilbon

Two beautiful waterfalls, an ancient Jewish village, a Syrian officer's swimming pool, and an old mill. A classic Golan river hike.

Route length: 6 km.
Difficulty: Family hike.
Start point: Gilbon Nature Reserve parking lot.
Access: Take the road leading up from Beit Hameches Junction. Beside kilometer marker 16, turn left on a dirt road marked in red.
End point: Shen Bridge, about 3 km north of Kibbutz Gadot (Route 918, between kilometer markers 18 and 19).
Duration: 4-5 hours (can be cut to 3).
Admission fees: None.
Opening hours: None.
Equipment: Bathing suit.
Remarks: Not recommended in the rainy season. Walk only on marked trails and paths – there are still many mine fields in the area!
Pickup point for cars: End of route.
Map: Golan and Hermon Hiking and Trail Map (No.1).

| jan | feb | mar | apr | may | jun | jul | aug | sep | oct | nov | dec |

En route to the parking lot of the Gilbon Nature Reserve, you'll pass the remains of the houses of the village of Aweinat el-Jenobiya. The village, like Aweinat es-Samalya, beside the parking lot, contains concrete buildings, built by the Syrian army prior to 1967, as well as traditional Golan-style buildings constructed of unhewn basalt stones with ceilings composed of poplar beams that rested on arches; the beams were covered with reed mats and coated with pressed earth. The eucalyptus tree groves around the villages were planted by the Syrian army in order to camouflage military activity in the villages and the Syrian outposts and bunkers around them.

Follow the red-marked dirt road to its end (turn right at the junction with the road marked in blue). The fenced areas around you, with little red triangles hanging on them, are Syrian mine fields. Most of them are used for grazing, with a cow vanishing every now and then. **Stay on the trails and do not climb over fences!** Park at the parking lot at the end of the road. The trail down to Nahal Gilbon, marked in red, starts between the houses. Follow the trail to the riverbed. Once across the river, you are at the top of the Devora Waterfall. Enjoy the view, but please, be careful.

Once across the river, you will arrive at a trail junction. Take the blue trail branching off to the north (right). It leads to Horvat Devora, the remains of the Syrian village of Daburiya. As you approach the ruins of the village, the trail makes its way through the remains of a major Syrian outpost. Many of the trenches and concrete bunkers are still intact between the eucalyptus trees on the slopes leading up to the village. The village buildings were all built of hewn basalt stones, with thatched roofs held up by stone arches and pillars. The stones for the buildings were taken from the remains of an ancient Jewish settlement on the site, referred to as Devora in Hebrew.

The Aramaic inscriptions carved into stones found on the site include one acknowledging the donation of a gate to a synagogue and another identifying a building as the religious academy of Rabbi Eleazar Hakapper (the caper maker). One lintel is decorated with a depiction of a bird of prey carrying a snake in its beak and accompanied by two fish. Images of palm trees were also found. The inscriptions and decorations indicate that this was the site of a Jewish settlement in Talmudic and Mishnaic times (Byzantine period). Rabbi Eleazar Hakapper and his academy are mentioned in the Talmud. The distance from the academy to the synagogue at Katzrin were given as an example for the distance that has to be covered in order to deem

shoes appropriate for wearing on the Sabbath. (Wearing new shoes on the Sabbath was not allowed.)

Return to the Devora Waterfall, which makes a 12-meter dive into a lovely pool. On the way to the bottom of the waterfall, you'll pass fig trees, olive trees, and prickly pear (*sabra*) hedges. Oleander bushes beside the pool bedeck the area with pink flowers in summer; giant reeds and lilac chaste trees grow beside the channel. The red trail continues down the river. One kilometer further down the riverbed is the 41-meter-high Gilbon Waterfall. In its basalt wall you can see lava flows from volcanic eruptions, and hexagonal pillars. View the waterfall from above (don't get too close to the edge of the cliff) and walk down the trail to the riverbed. Walk upriver for 50 meters to reach the beautiful pool at the bottom of the waterfall. Rock doves and hawks nest in the cliff face of the waterfall.

From the pool you can take a shortcut back to the starting point by retracing your steps along the red trail. Climb the steep slope back to the observation area. Near the top, a blue-marked trail leads off to the the right, up the steep slope. After a strenuous climb, you will reach the Gilbon Waterfall picnic area. From here, follow the unpaved road, marked in blue, back to the junction with the road marked in red. Turn left and follow the red road to the parking area where you started the hike.

Otherwise, continue from the waterfall for another 2.5 km along the red trail to the spring of Ein Gilbon. Before reaching the spring, the trail leaves the riverbed and makes its way around the ruins of Al Jalabina. **Do not leave the trail as there are mine fields around it!** The waters of Ein Gilbon used to collect in a pool frequented by Syrian soldiers and therefore known as one of the Golan's "Officers' Pools." Many years ago, the pool's wall was broken intentionally so that the water wouldn't fill it any more. Even so, a dip in the freezing water is still a treat after a few hours' walk.

From the southwestern side of the pool, the path continues down the slope into the Hula Valley. A 10-minute walk down the path will bring you to the remains of a flour mill that is hidden among the trees. Water pours down from the tall channel that used to supply the power for the mill. Walking a few hundred meters more will bring you to an unpaved road that is marked in red. Follow the road to the Shen bridge over the Jordan River. The bridge is also known as "Gesher Hapekak" (Cork Bridge) because it was at this point that the Hula Lake was drained — the cork that stopped the Jordan from flowing to the Sea of Galilee was pulled out. Your car should be waiting at the bridge.

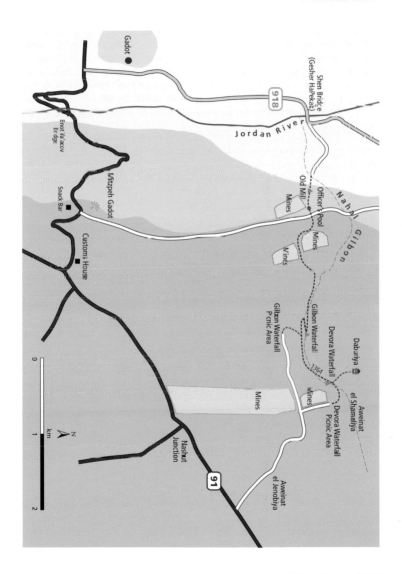

Route 04:

The White and Black Waterfalls of Nahal El Al

The whole family will enjoy this classic Golan hike, which includes two waterfalls, vultures, and amazing views.

Route length: 7 km.
Difficulty: Easy to moderate.
Start point: Nahal El Al parking lot.
Access: From approach road to Moshav Eliad.
End point: Ring route.
Duration: 3 hours.
Admission fees: None.
Opening hours: None.
Equipment: Regular.
Remarks: To shorten the hike, you can follow the trail to Avnei Eitan and be picked up there.
Pickup point for cars: End of route.
Map: Golan and Hermon Hiking and Trail Map (No 1).

jan feb mar apr may jun jul aug sep oct nov dec

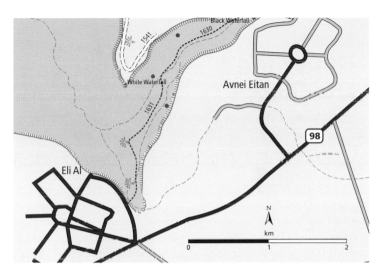

Start the tour at the Nahal El Al parking lot, which is on the approach road to Moshav Eliad in the Golan. Take the red-marked trail (1631) that leads down the steps and into the canyon of Nahal El Al. The trail makes its way through the remains of the orchards and fields of a Syrian village that used to stand here.

After about 1 kilometer, the trail begins to descend into the riverbed of Nahal El Al. The White Waterfall can be seen in the distance in the canyon.

The trail descends to the riverbed above the waterfall. A branch of the trail leads to the pool below the waterfall.

Continue on the red-marked trail (1630), walking upriver to the Black Waterfall, which cascades over black basalt rocks, hence its name.

From here, you can retrace your steps to the parking lot. Alternatively, you can continue on the red-marked trail, which ends in Moshav Avnei Eitan. From here, either have a car pick you up or walk to the main road and back to the parking lot (a 4-km walk that in any case takes less time than the hike back up the canyon).

Route 05:
Upper Nahal Zavitan

One of the coolest places to be in Israel in summer is the Golan, especially in the cold spring waters of Nahal Zavitan.

Route length: 8 km.

Difficulty: Moderate. Suitable for families of able hikers.

Start point: The red-marked trail along the riverbed begins beside Route 9088, 2 km east of Katzrin. From Katzrin's SPNI field school, there are also unmarked trails and a jeep track that will lead you through a cow pasture to the same red trail. Consult your trail map.

Access: From Route 87.

End point: Yehudiya campsite along Route 87.

Duration: All day, if you linger at the pools.

Admission fees: None.

Opening hours: None.

Equipment: Three liters of water per person and wading shoes.

Remarks: Don't jump into the pools. Bathing in the pools is dangerous, swimming is at your own risk.

Pickup point for cars: End of route.

Map: Golan and Hermon Hiking and Trail Map (No. 1).

| jan | feb | mar | apr | may | jun | jul | aug | sep | oct | nov | dec |

The rivers of the central Golan Heights flow into steep canyons that make a spectacular descent into the Jordan Valley and the Sea of Galilee. In the riverbeds, an abundance of springs, pools, and waterfalls can be found. This tour will take you to one of the most popular of these canyons, the upper part of Nahal Zavitan.

Begin the hike at the start of the red-marked trail (No. 1451) in the small parking area on the road to Katzrin. The parking area is easy to find: From the Katzrin junction on Route 87, turn towards Katzrin. After a few hundred meters the road makes a sharp turn to the left and descends into the riverbed of Nahal Zavitan. The parking lot is on your left at the point where the road crosses the riverbed.

After 1.5 km of walking, you'll begin to hear the water flowing along the stream. The name of the river stems from its Arabic name: Zawitan, which means angles, a name derived from the polygonal columns that are created by the basalt rocks along the riverbed. Unlike many of the riverbeds on the Golan, the water here flows in ample quantities all year long, nourishing oleander, willow trees, bramble bushes, and freshwater crabs. In the cliffs, which gradually rise higher as you proceed along the trail, vultures, eagles, and small mammals thrive.

Two kilometers further down, you'll pass a series of pools, known for the polygonal basalt formations that protrude from the sides. Walk another kilometer along the trail to reach the 33-meter-high Zavitan Waterfall. Enjoy the view from the trail, above the waterfall. At the trail junction, take the blue-marked trail down to the pool. The ladder here will help you negotiate the steep descent. The pool is a good spot for a break. The water is cold all year round, even in the height of summer, and the trees and bushes around offer ample shade. **(Do not dive into the water. It is cold and full of rocks!)**

After enjoying yourself at the pool, climb back up to the red trail and turn right, continuing south on the path, which runs along the top of a spectacular basalt canyon known as the "Black Canyon." The canyon can only be descended with the aid of ropes, something which should not be attempted without an experienced guide. The canyon has taken its toll in lives of careless hikers. In the distance, the Sea of Galilee can be clearly seen.

The trail passes through a grove of Mount Tabor oaks and plum trees. These

Zavitan Waterfall.

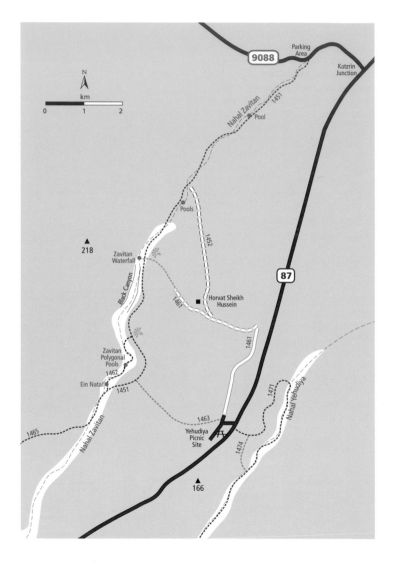

are part of the Yehudiya Forest, which covers the central Golan and is one of the few surviving patches of the huge forests that once covered the Golan and Galilee. It is a typical Mediterranean park forest with large grass-covered spaces between the trees. A large number of gazelles graze in the forest area and can be easily spotted among the trees or the grassy meadows. The area is also home to a number of other large mammals like wild boars and wolves; don't worry, sightings of boars and wolves are rarer than sightings of gazelles.

About 2.5 km further on, the trail reaches a junction with a trail marked in black. The red trail continues along the crest of the riverbed canyon. The black trail descends down to the riverbed and will take you to the "Zavitan Polygon Pools"

and the spring of Ein Nataf. At this point, you have two options. You can either descend to the pools with the trail marked in black or continue with the trail along the riverbed to the spring of Ein Nataf. At the spring, you will meet up again with the red trail. Take the red trail back (left) up the slope of the riverbed to the junction with the trail marked in green. The hike along the riverbed is strenuous and not easy. **(This part of the hike is for good hikers and not a family hike.)**

The second option is to continue along the trail marked in red along the top of the canyon, until you come to the junction with a trail marked in green.

The green trail will lead you, after 2 km, to the Yehudiya picnic site, which is where our route ends.

Fox in the Yehudiya Forest.

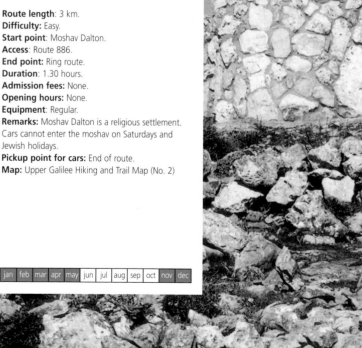

Route 06:
Rabbi Yossi Hagalili's Neighborhood

Graves of ancient Jewish sages abound in the Galilee. Follow this fun hike to visit some of the lesser-known graves. The view is an added bonus.

Route length: 3 km.
Difficulty: Easy.
Start point: Moshav Dalton.
Access: Route 886.
End point: Ring route.
Duration: 1.30 hours.
Admission fees: None.
Opening hours: None.
Equipment: Regular.
Remarks: Moshav Dalton is a religious settlement. Cars cannot enter the moshav on Saturdays and Jewish holidays.
Pickup point for cars: End of route.
Map: Upper Galilee Hiking and Trail Map (No. 2)

| jan | feb | mar | apr | may | jun | jul | aug | sep | oct | nov | dec |

From the entrance to Moshav Dalton, follow the signs and drive to the grave of Rabbi Yossi Hagalili at the top of Mount Dalton. The signs will lead you to the back gate of the moshav and along a road leading up to the summit. Yossi Hagalili was a Galilean Jewish sage who lived during the second century. Like the Mishnaic sage known as Honi the Circlemaker, Yossi Hagalili was regarded as a rainmaker. His grave at Dalton is mentioned in a report from 910 CE by the Karaite, Sahal ben Matzliah. According to this tenth-century document, it was customary for childless women to pray at the grave. The grave remains a popular pilgrimage site. Every summer, on Tu Be'av (15th of Av), the festival of courtship and love, a local celebration is held at the site.

Return by car along the same route. Just after the back gate, make a left into the moshav and drive along the security fence until you see another exit leading eastward. The exit is marked with signs directing you to the graves of Yishmael ben Yossi Hagalili and Yehuda ben Timma.

Follow the paved road, which has red trail markings (2155). After passing the cemetery, you'll come to signs leading to the grave of Rabbi Yishmael. Park and go up to the grave, which is in a little whitewashed compound graced by an olive tree. It is on the left side of the road. You can also get here by foot from Yossi Hagalili's grave by walking down the south face of Mount Dalton, past the remains of the village of Dalta. Medieval sources state that the grave of Rabbi Yishmael, son of Yossi Hagalili, is at Dalton. This reference is problematic, however. Yossi Hagalili's son was Rabbi Eliezer; Rabbi Yishmael is related to Abba Halafta.

After visiting the grave, you can continue by car along the red-marked dirt road until

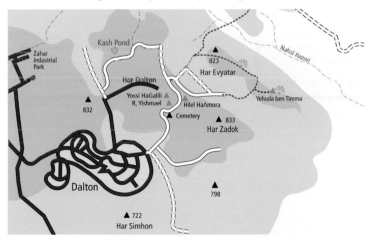

it curves to the right, leading you to an apple orchard. Park here, off the road. Look around until you find the green trail markings painted on the orchard's fence posts. Follow the markings through a cow pasture. At the far end of the pasture you might see a tame-looking little fox. The fox has become accustomed to human visitors and expects to be fed. As foxes are known carriers of rabies, keep a safe distance from this wild animal. The green trail ends at a junction with a red trail. Turn right along the red trail (2156), and go up Mount Evyatar. The trail winds through the brush and bushes, and you might lose sight of the markings every now and then. Patience and a quick search or careful backtracking will keep you on the path. Once atop the mountain, you'll have a spectacular view of the Alma Plateau, the Nahal Dishon

riverbed, the northern border settlements, and the Hula Valley. In winter, wildflowers bloom in abundance on this hill, among them the rare wild hyacinth, which is dark blue. Follow the red trail eastward along the mountain. At the point where the path turns south, just past a small clump of trees, you'll come to a signposted path that leads to the grave of Yehuda ben Timma. The grave is 150 meters inside a military firing range area. Hikers and pilgrims still enter the area, but be aware that you are doing so at your own risk. Yehuda ben Timma was a second-century Galilean sage, his grave in Dalton was mentioned by the sixteenth-century Jewish traveller Moshe Basula, who visited the area in 1522.

After that, continue along the red trail back to the orchard. Turn right along the red trail markings and back to your car.

Route 07:
Yiftah Canyon to Goma Junction

One of the most beautiful spring hikes in Israel. This route descends the 800-meter-high Naftali range cliff into the Hula Valley, offering spectacular views of Mount Hermon, the Golan, and Lebanon.

Route length: 6 km.
Difficulty: Family hike.
Start point: Route 886, between kilometer markers 65 and 66.
Access: From Yiftah Junction.
End point: Route 90, near Goma Junction.
Duration: 4 hours.
Admission fees: None.
Opening hours: None.
Equipment: Regular.
Remarks: Spectacular family hike during the late winter or early spring (March-May). Be careful getting out of the car at the start point; approaching cars driving round the bend on the road can't see you!
Pickup point for cars: End of route.
Map: Golan and Hermon Hiking and Trail Map (No. 1).

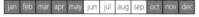

jan feb mar apr may jun jul aug sep oct nov dec

This six-kilometer route is a great spring walk down a breathtaking mountainside. The trail leads down the Naftali Mountain Range straight into the Hula Valley. In April and early May, wild hyacinths, anemones, and tulips are in full bloom all around.

Drive north on Route 886 past Kibbutz Yiftah, until you come to kilometer markers 65 and 66. To the right along this stretch of road, you'll see an opening in the fence along the road with a wide path leading through it.

This is where you should begin your descent on foot into the Yiftah Canyon.

Park carefully. There is no parking area here and the road is dangerous. As the tour ends at the Goma Junction, you will need to arrange for a driver to pick you up there.

The canyon is actually a chasm jumbled up with rocks. Small metal grips allow for a fun time while climbing through. Explore – it will take longer than you think. The chasm continues on the other side of the road. From the canyon, a trail marked in blue (trail 2060) leads off into the woods. Follow it to a paved road that leads to a farm further down the slope.

Continue following the blue trail markings as they lead you along the road down the hill to a point where the trail leaves the road. Descend here along a wooded slope to a gate in a fence.

Go through the gate, but please make sure to close it afterward. The trail curls around a hill. The top of the hill has a few farm buildings on it.

Suddenly, you will reach the edge of the

Entrance to Yiftah Canyon.

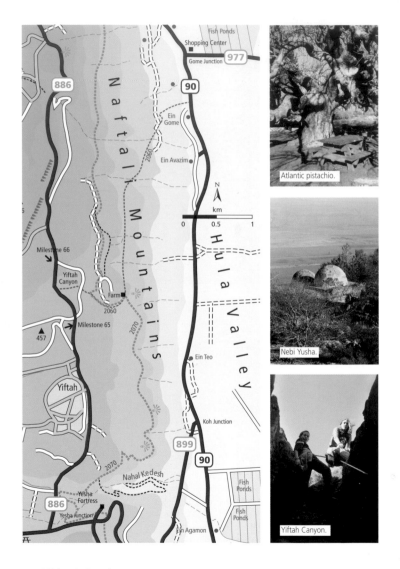

Atlantic pistachio.

Nebi Yusha.

Yiftah Canyon.

Mediterranean woods.

cliff face that drops off into the Hula Valley. Find a spot to stop and enjoy the view here with its fish ponds, channels, and new flooded areas called the "Agamon" (the small lake). Opposite is the Golan Heights, with its two lines of volcanoes clearly visible. Snow-capped Mount Hermon looms in the distance, with the Lebanon Valley and the mountains of Lebanon further back.

The trail goes along the cliff for awhile and then begins to descend into the Hula Valley. At first, it follows a course through natural woods, planted pine forests, and heavy scrub. In May, the flowers, bushes, and trees on the slope burst into various shades of yellow. The ground is covered with the best, and the rarest, of Israel's wild flowers.

Large oak trees and ancient Atlantic pistachios dot the path. They are the last remains of the ancient forests of Naftali. The trail ends at Route 90, beside kilometer marker 464, near the Goma Junction.

Route 08:
Keshet to Sharach

A hike between two very different caves in the limestone formations of the Upper Galilee. One is a collapsed rainbow cave in a cliff, the other is a warren of karst tunnels.

Route length: 7.6 km.
Difficulty: Easy-Moderate.
Start point: Adamit picnic site, west of Horvat Adamit.
Access: From Shlomi, drive east on the Northern Border Road (Route 899) and turn left onto the access road to Kibbutz Adamit. Continue 4 more km in the direction of the kibbutz, turning right on an unpaved road marked in green that ends at the JNF's Adamit picnic site, where the trail begins.
End point: Sharach Picnic Site, 100 meters west of the entrance to Granot Hagalil. Walk 1 km on the blue-marked unpaved road to the parking area.
Duration: 7 hours.
Admission fees: None.
Opening hours: None.
Equipment: Flashlight.
Remarks: If you want a shorter route (4 km), start your hike at Kibbutz Eilon and descend along a kibbutz back road to the pumping station and Karkara Springs. Follow the trail to the Sharach Cave.
Pickup point for cars: End of route.
Map: Upper Galilee Hiking and Trail Map (No. 2).

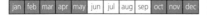

| jan | feb | mar | apr | may | jun | jul | aug | sep | oct | nov | dec |

From Adamit Park, begin hiking on the green-marked trail (No. 2180 on the trail map). The beginning of the trail is paved in order to allow wheelchair access to the Keshet Cave. The cave's walls and roof have collapsed, leaving only a huge limestone arch still intact, from which the cave's Hebrew name, Keshet (arch) derives. The top of the arch is a popular jumping off point for rappellers, who can thus descend some 30 meters along the exposed cliff face before landing on the firm ground of the former cave floor. There's a good chance that on arrival at the cave you'll see a few Spiderman-like types roaming around.

From this lookout point, high up on the side of a hill, you will also have a lovely view of the coastal region and the Upper Galilee, the Haifa Bay, the Carmel Range to the south and west, and the Nahal Bet-zet riverbed in the valley below.

A look down at the goat dung on the floor of the cave will tell you in a minute that generations of shepherds, right up until modern times, have used the cave for shelter from pouring rain and sweltering heat. After inspecting the cave, follow the ridge of the cliff eastward on the red-marked trail (2207). The trail passes to the south of Kibbutz Adamit and 3 km later descends into the riverbed of Nahal Bet-zet. At the junction of the blue trail (2206) and the red trail, turn left. The trail here is shaded by large oriental plane trees. In Israel's hot climate, these trees need plenty of water. They grow happily along this riverbed, where water flows all year long from the Karkara Springs, which feed a number of shallow pools further down the blue trail. Follow the trail through the large oleander bushes that

Keshet Cave.

Khirbet Adamit.

bloom in pink in summer.

Continue along the trail for another kilometer up the riverbed. At this point, Nahal Betzet flows through an impressive wide canyon with 300-meter-high limestone cliffs on both sides. The cliff face is pockmarked with caves and cavities, typical of limestone rocks in a land with abundant winter rains. The trail crosses the riverbed and reaches a fork in the canyon. Here you come to a trail junction. The black trail leads to the Bedouin village of Arab el-Aramshe at the top of the Adamit range. We will follow the blue trail, that leads off to the right. The trail (2206) now enters Nahal Sharach and leads through Mediterranean woods, which are replete with common oaks, pistachio trees, officinal storax, Judas trees, and ivy. The whole area is also laced with ferns (*sharach* in Hebrew), after which the riverbed and cave are named. The lush overgrowth makes this a cool hike, even on a hot day.

Half a kilometer after the fork in the riverbed, you'll see the Sharach Cave on your left. Take a flashlight and enter the cave, observing the stalactite formations created by water seeping through the calcium carbonate of the cave walls. The Israel Nature and Parks Authority has marked a short walking route through the narrow cave, complete with a ladder; you'll exit from a second opening that is a bit to the east.

Continue along the blue trail, past the cave, for about 1.5 km along a gentle uphill incline. You'll emerge from the woods into the JNF Sharach picnic site.

Headed Thyme.

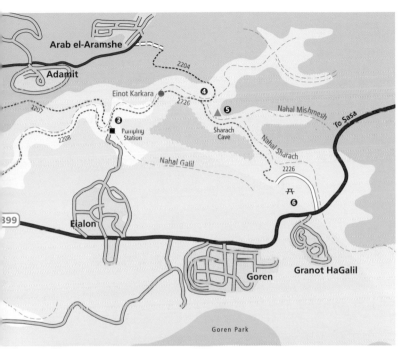

Adamit lookout.

The Brilliance of Mount Meron

Countless holy people have found shelter on the slopes of Mt. Meron. The graves of the righteous dot the refreshing green landscape and ancient synagogues abound amidst the beauty of the Mediterranean forest. A route for experienced hikers leads from the grave of Rabbi Shimon Bar Yochai to the Elkosh Bridge by Hurfeish.

Route length: 22 km.
Difficulty: Good hikers.
Start point: Meron campground by Nahal Meron.
Access: Between kilometer markers 41 and 42 on Route 866 (Hananiya Junction to Meron Junction).
End point: Elkosh Bridge just west of Hurfeish.
Duration: 10 hours.
Admission fees: None.
Opening hours: None.
Equipment: Regular.
Remarks: It's difficult to find water along the route other than at the Sarteva Spring. Bring 4 liters of water per person.
Pickup point for cars: End of route.
Map: Upper Galilee Hiking and Trail Map (No. 2).

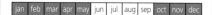

jan feb mar apr may jun jul aug sep oct nov dec

The campground by the riverbed of Nahal Meron is an excellent starting point for a hike. The only problem with this campground is that it lies in the only bend on Route 866, which ascends from Parod to Meron, and so it only can be accessed from one side of the road – the side leading from Meron. Other than that, everything else is ideal. There are tables, drinking water, a spring, and even shade from the trees at the campground.

Start the hike from the beginning of the blue trail, which runs alongside the riverbed. After roughly 200 meters, ascend the slope on the right along the trail marked in black, which leads to the grave of Rabbi Shimon Bar Yochai. Since this hike is a long one, it is best to visit the grave at another time and continue to the parking area beside the yeshiva. A sharp eye can discern that, just at the point where a paved road leaves the parking lot, an old staircase twists to the left. This is the site of the ancient Meron synagogue, an important spot to visit, even in our limited time.

This synagogue was built in the third century to serve the Jews of Meron. The builders made good use of the natural rock, turning it into the synagogue's western wall and floor. The facade, which is still intact, has three openings and its simple decorations complement the area's landscape. Behind the facade are both remains of and signs of the bases of the pillars that once stood here. According to a local legend, the Messiah will arrive when the cracked lintel above the doorway of the synagogue falls. Since there is no lack of signs that the Messiah will turn up any day now, the lintel has been reinforced.

The synagogue rests on an elevated rock platform, providing a view of the graves of the righteous that are scattered here in abundance. Since our time is short, just take a quick look, descend again to the path, and hike northward about 500 meters, until the gate of the fence that extends along the left side of the path. Beside the gate there is a wicket that marks the beginning of the path. This path leads through a wonderful grove with everything that you could wish for in a grove: moss in the shadowy places and grasses and flowers (that blossom late in the spring).

When you leave the grove, the view of the green slope of Mt. Meron blocks the sky. The climb upwards to bypass the saddle that separates Mt. Meron and Mt. Bar Yochai looks like a suicidal feat, but the black marked trail was created during the British Mandate, when the natural outline of the landscape was respected. The result is a path, which is reinforced with low walls at some points, that overcomes the great divide of almost 400 meters with much logic and patience. So, the going is not difficult at all.

During the climb, the view is gradually revealed (providing a great excuse for a stop now and again). At the foot of Mt. Meron is Moshav Meron and beside it are two small settlements: Bar Yochai and Or Ganuz. There also is a great view of Gush Halav and what used to be Sifsufa (the residents lobbied to change its name to Kfar Hoshen). You also see Mt. Puah and Kibbutz Baram. Higher up, you can spot Safed, Mt. Hermon, Ramat Dalton, and the large drainage basin of the Dishon River, which drains the eastern part of the Meron Mountains. Unfortunately, the greenery here was scarred by the Second Lebanon War. Many of the rockets the Hizbullah fired landed in this area and caused forest fires.

The point where the forest of Kermes oaks is joined by eastern strawberry trees (*Arbutus andrachne* in Latin) is a sign that we are hiking on marl. Unsurprisingly, trailblazers also like this soft rock and so we will cross it and continue straight ahead to the trail with black markings, across from the green slope of Mt. Meron.

It is a pleasant climb until we reach the campground of Shvil Hapisga, which is located between Mt. Meron and Mt. Bar Yochai, some 1,140 meters above sea level. This is also the borderline between different sections of the nation's water supply. Until now, we were in the drainage basin of Nahal Amud, which flows into the Sea of Galilee. From now on, we will hike along the drainage basin of Nahal Keziv, which flows into the Mediterranean Sea.

From here, there is not much climbing left because we are almost at the highest point in the Galilee. Our path (with blue trail markings) joins the Israel Trail briefly and continues straight between the parking lot and the picnic tables of the camping ground. After passing some oaks, we will part company with the Israel Trail and continue along the trail with blue markings. It runs along the ridge that separates Nahal Ofa'im (on the right) and Nahal Zeved (on the left). Nahal Ofa'im is closed to hikers in order to allow the surrounding woods to develop undisturbed. Across from us, at the base of Mt. Ofa'im, is the Forester's House. This structure, which is no longer in use, was built when the British Mandate surveyed the forest.

At the foot of Mt. Ofa'im lies the ruins of the Bek community, demarcated by four walnut trees and an old eastern strawberry tree. The remains of the buildings bear witness to the trials experienced by the pioneering settlement established by Rabbi Israel Bek, who immigrated from Berdichev in 1832. After Bek healed the Turkish governor, who presided over the region from Acre, the governor expressed his gratitude by giving Bek a parcel of land adjacent to Kafr Jermak. In 1836, Bek established an agricultural settlement here. His son, Nissan, ran the farm, and five Hasidic families joined him from Safed. However, the residents of Bek did not get along with the residents of the area and so the newcomers abandoned the settlement in 1840.

It is worth wandering a little bit around the ruins. On the slope under the walnut trees, in addition to the remains of Bek, we found remains of an ancient settlement that included rock carvings, a columbarium, and an oil press. Nearby is a small spring called Be'er Rom.

The trail cuts through the ruins and arrives at marl stairs covered with orchids. The broad-leaved helleborine, a rare member of the orchid family, grows here in mid-April and May. It is easy to recognize – its deep, dark blossom holds generous amounts of nectar that attracts insects.

The trail then leads past a large, exposed cliff that is some 300 meters long, and a dirt road. If you want to see the entrance to Jermak's Huta, turn left onto the dirt road and walk for about five minutes. The word huta is a nickname that hikers use to describe large pits formed by water eating into soft rock over many years. The pits can be dozens of meters deep. Huta probably is a bastardization of the Arabic word *hawa*, which means abyss.

There's an iron fence in front of the entrance to Jermak's Huta to prevent careless hikers from falling into the 150-meter-deep pit. There are many fables about this pit. In Beit Jann, they say that in Ottoman times, the residents of the village refused to pay taxes and would throw the tax collectors down the pit. When the local governor in Safed realized that the tax collectors were disappearing, he sent his soldiers to find them. The soldiers soon discovered what was happening and in retaliation raided the nearby village of Jermak and threw all of the residents they caught into the pit. And that, according to the fable, was the end of the village of Jermak.

Jermak's Huta contains stalactites, stalagmites, fissures, and caverns. Rare species of bats have been discovered here, including the long-fingered, greater horseshoe, serotine, and common pipistrelle. In order to protect both the natural environment and the visitors, entry is prohibited.

After taking a look, return to the trail with blue markings. Take a look at the beautiful winepress to the right of the trail; the area for stomping the grapes and the two pools that the fresh juice ran into are clearly discernable.

From here, the path descends toward Nahal Keziv. The path crosses through some agricultural areas before reaching the riverbed of Nahal Zeved, just before it merges with Nahal Keziv. We enter the riverbed, turn right, and walk in it until we reach Nahal Keziv. It is very easy to recognize Nahal Keziv thanks to the sewage and turbid water that flow into it from Beit Jann. We cross the river and climb the slope a little (following the blue trail markings). The map also shows a path with black markings here, but the markings for it are difficult to find; many have been moved or destroyed due to the frequently changing borders of agricultural plots. Therefore, we ascend a few more meters and turn right on the first dirt road, which descends in parallel to the river and meets it later. Anyone who is thirsty or suffering from dehydration can continue walking upward on the blue marked trail for another three minutes to reach the Sarteva Spring.

The black-marked trail takes us through difficult terrain – agricultural terraces built from huge boulders. They were piled one on top of the other with mechanical tools. The trail ends at the road connecting the Druze villages of Hurfeish and Beit Jann, both of which are located in the Mt. Meron Nature Reserve.

The building of this narrow road was the subject of a lengthy battle between the villages' residents and the Israel Nature and Parks Authority (INPA) and other environmental groups. The road runs through the Nahal Keziv channel in order to link the villages. Before the road was paved, it took 40 minutes to drive from one village to the other – you had to drive out to the main highway, follow the highway to the turnoff for the other village, and then drive all the way back to the other village. In the

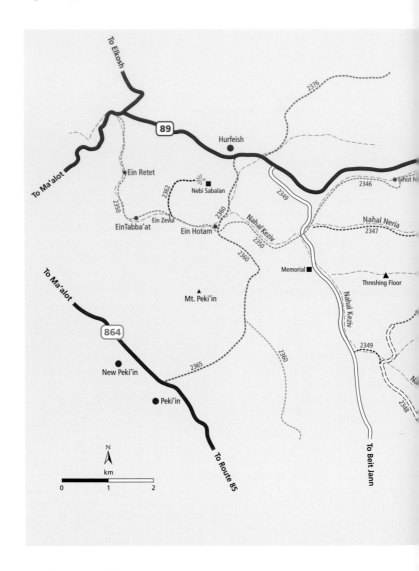

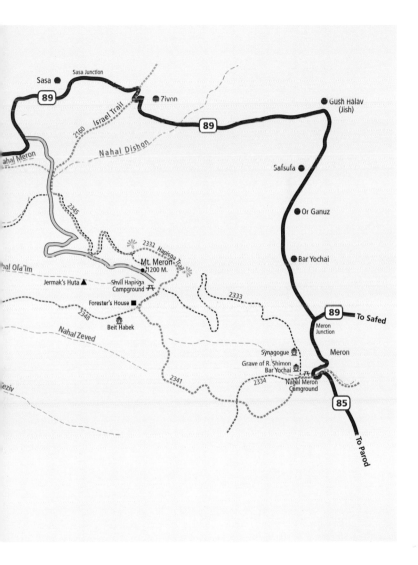

1990s, the residents paved the road under cover of night, without a permit and against the will of the INPA. The battle involved violence, threats, and court orders, but the residents had the upper hand from the start.

The terraces and the road tell the story of the conflict that exists between the residents and the INPA, which is responsible for the nature reserve. The residents of Beit Jann, along with a few others from Hurfeish, Ein el-Asad, and Peki'in, own about 20,000 dunams (5,000 acres) of land within the reserve. The land is greatly spread out and is used for a variety of activities. Farming, building infrastructure for roads, hunting, and other activities at all hours of the day and night, as well as fires, cause great damage to the natural environment. The INPA invests vast efforts to reduce the toll this takes on the environment. INPA staff members mapped the most important areas to preserve and are negotiating a land swap with the residents. The idea is that the residents will receive agricultural land in exchange for land located in the areas that are important to preserve.

In addition to the obvious benefits to nature, the residents would benefit since they would not have to invest in developing the land for agriculture. The process of implementing a land swap is long and complicated; mutual suspicion makes the process even more difficult. However, the only way to solve most of the problems in the Mt. Meron Nature Reserve is to concentrate the land slated for preservation in one area under one authority.

We hike northward on the road for 2.5 kilometers. On the way, we pass the monument that some residents erected in memory of the 73 soldiers killed when two IDF helicopters collided in this area in 1997. The monuments too play a role in the battle here. They are often built in order to strengthen the residents' claim on certain areas so that they will be excluded from the land swaps.

Nahal Ofa'im comes from the right and descends into Nahal Keziv. On the north bank of the riverbed, not far from the road, we can see the Rikson Ruins – ancient terraces and the remains of structures from the Ottoman period. Beit Jann residents used to reside there during the farming season.

Just after the riverbeds meet, follow the green trail markings and then turn left along Nahal Keziv. Between here and the Elkosh Bridge, we pass more than a few cows, who enjoy chomping on the grasses by Nahal Keziv.

We soon reach Ein Hotam (Ein Elmazarib), which flows from a small structure with a carved opening leading to a large basin. Beside it, a tiny stream flows from a crevice in the rock and into the same basin. A large terebinth tree grows out of the same crevice.

The rest of the path is an easy stretch. As we walk, we see the sewage water from Beit Jann trickle across the earth until it is absorbed. We also see clearer water that bursts forth from time to time in the channel, creating springs such as Ein Zevul, Ein Retet, and Ein Tabba'at. We continue on to the Elkosh Bridge, which is adjacent to the Hurfeish soccer field and is the end point of our hike.

Rockrose in full bloom.

Trail marking.

Nahal Keziv.

Ancient Meron synagogue.

Route 10:
The Rock of Akhbara

Hikers have somehow overlooked the Rock of Akhbara reserve, even though a clearly marked trail passes alongside this wonderful cliff. Once upon a time, it was a popular nesting ground for vultures, but today they have almost abandoned it. Don't let that dissuade you – it has a great view and an interesting history.

Route length: 6 km.
Difficulty: Easy.
Start point: The dirt road that leads eastward before the first house of Akhbara.
Access: From Akhbara Bridge on Route 89.
End point: Ein Sela or the Parod-Amiad Highway (Route 85) beside kilometer marker 40.
Duration: 2-3 hours to Ein Sela, 3-4 hours to the Parod-Amiad Highway, 3-4 hours from Ein Sela back to Akhbara.
Admission fees: None.
Opening hours: None.
Equipment: Regular.
Remarks: Experienced hikers can continue from the end of the route by foot to the lower section of Nahal Amud until the Hukuk Highway, an easy nine-kilometer hike along the Israel Trail that passes the famous pillar that gives the riverbed its name.
Pickup point for cars: She'ar Yashuv bridge. Buses should wait for hikers at the edge of the moshav.
Map: Upper Galilee Hiking and Trail Map (No. 2).

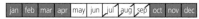
jan | feb | mar | apr | may | jun | jul | aug | sep | oct | nov | dec

From the edge of the Oranim Forest of Ramat Pashur, the cliff of the Rock of Akhbara reserve can be seen in all its glory: a kilometer and a half long, the cliff rises 150 meters above the channel of the Nahal Akhbara riverbed. In the afternoon, when the sun shines directly on the reddish stone, every entrance to the many caves in it can be clearly seen.

In the 1990s, 16 pairs of vultures nested here, according to Israel Nature and Parks Authority ranger Khaled Heleyhel. A resident of the nearby village of Akhbara, he has been monitoring the vulture population here for years. The times he is talking about seem like ancient history today. This year only one pair of vultures nested here, but they soon drew the same conclusion as the others and left after only two weeks.

What is happening at the Rock of Akhbara reserve is typical of the vulture population in the Galilee in general. There was a relatively successful nesting season at the Ein Seter cliff in the Nahal Amud riverbed that resulted in two chicks, Heleyhel says. However, it had an unhappy end. One of the chicks disappeared in mysterious circumstances plus one of its parents died of poisoning.

"Buzzards have followed the vultures to nest here and in the plum trees in the riverbed you can see short-toed eagle nests," Heleyhel says. "This year we also saw a red falcon flying in the area, though it did not nest in the reserve. There is an abundance of rock hares, deer ramble along the slopes, and occasionally you come across a wild boar, porcupine, or badger. My house overlooks the cliff. Sometimes I just sit and observe it, but I never see vultures anymore — only rock."

Only rock means a lot when you are talking about the Rock of Akhbara, as you can discover on a short hike along the path that runs along the foot of the cliff.

The new highway between Rosh Pina and Safed has made life easier for the residents of Akhbara. This major highway, a bit west of the largest bridge in Israel, extends to Nahal Akhbara and to the village. The newer buildings are part of "the new village," which has been part of the Safed municipality since 1979. On the other side of Nahal Akhbara is the abandoned "old village." The remains of its stone buildings are mainly used to house sheep nowadays. The current residents of Akhbara are refugees from the Arab villages of the Galilee who gathered there after Akhbara's original residents abandoned it during the War of Independence. The myrtle that can be found growing between buildings in both parts is considered especially high quality and is often used in lulavs for the Sukkot festival.

A short dirt road, marked in blue, leads south toward a hiking trail marked in blue. The path passes along the eastern edge of the new village, crosses the paved road, and, at the large carob tree, turns toward the riverbed. It is worth taking a slight detour here to check out the old village, believed to be the site of the town of Akhbara mentioned in the Mishna and Talmud. A Jewish community existed here until the eleventh century.

The stone houses standing here today are built from stones taken from older buildings. Moses Basula, who passed through here in 1522, identified the

remains of a synagogue. "At the heights of the village are the ruins of a synagogue," he wrote. "Two of the walls that were constructed from large stones are still three cubits high, as Rabbi Shimon bar Yochai built them." Basula's conjecture that bar Yochai built the synagogue was based on the tradition that his son, Rabbi Eliezer, lived in Akhbara.

In the 1980s, Dr. Zvi Ilan, who specialized in identifying ancient synagogues, found part of the eastern wall of a structure in the upper part of the village. It was made of carved stone blocks, like those used in ancient synagogues. Other architectural details were found nearby, but most of the synagogue is still waiting to be uncovered by archaeologists.

A family lives in one of the houses on the edge of the old town — the amazing view the location provides of the Rock of Akhbara outweighs the solitude.

Before leaving the old village, head southward on the slope, between the prickly pear bushes, toward Nahal Akhbara. The shepherds' paths lead past two domed roofs painted blue, one of which is made of natural rock. They mark what is believed to be the grave of Rabbi Yannai, who had a seminary in Akhbara. The gravestone itself is also painted blue and is located inside a building shaded by two European nettle trees and a mulberry tree. A spring completes the picturesque scene here.

Rabbi Yannai lived at the time of Rabbi Akiva. Among the various sayings attributed to him, one stands out: "The tranquility of the evil and the agony of the righteous do not lie in our hands." For we ordinary mortals cannot think of ourselves either as complete sinners who are beyond all hope or as absolute saints who have already fulfilled all of the commandments.

After checking out the village, return to the trail and continue along the right bank of Nahal Akhbara. There are fish in the river in the summer, but the main attraction here is the great cliff that the path passes underneath. Slightly to the north of a small spring called Ein Yannai are ancient remains that may be the village of Ukeba mentioned in the Mishna and Talmud.

It is also worth taking a look at the winding slope at the northern edge of the cliff. The structure with the domed roofs that can be seen from here is said to contain the graves of Rabbi Akiva ben Mahalal and

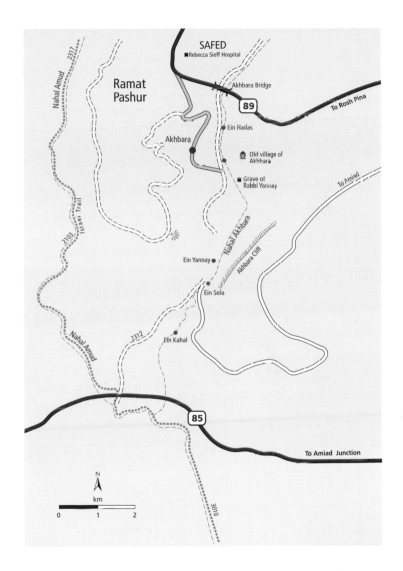

SAFED
■ Rebecca Sieff Hospital

Nahal Amud

2317

Ramat
Pashur

Akhbara Bridge

To Rosh Pina

89

Ein Hadas

Akhbara

Old village of
Akhbara

Grave of
Rabbi Yannay

To Amiad

Israel Trail

2103

Nahal Akhbara

Ein Yannay

Akhbara Cliff

Ein Sela

Nahal Amud

2312

Ein Kahal

85

To Amiad Junction

N

km

0   1   2

3010

Rabbi Admon ben Gadai.

After passing an impressive Atlantic pistachio tree, the path descends to the Ein Sela spring. A small stream flows down the riverbed. Some old, thick-trunked olive trees grow alongside.

Near the spring are ruins that are marked on old maps as Hirbat al-Hakab. The name is apparently a distortion of the Arabic name Akab, which means "a path through the mountains." The spring's current name, Ein Sela, does not do the place justice. First of all, it is likely that this is the location of Sela Akhbara, one of the fortresses that Josephus Flavius built in preparation for the Great Revolt against the Romans. Second, a little further on above the river, lie huge boulders that fell from the cliff.

Ein Sela is not the only confusing name here. At the end of the Middle Ages, the spring was called Ein Kahal. At the same time, a tradition developed, whose source apparently was the mystics of Safed, that the cliff above the spring was one of the places where the treasures of the Temple were hidden. This too was a distortion of earlier writings, which mention a spring called Ein Katal where the Temple treasures were hidden. The Government Names Committees did not give up on the name Kahal, however, and gave it to another spring that is located further along the slope of the river.

Persistent rumors tell that the tradition

The Rock of Akhbara.

about the Temple treasures reached the ears of the officers of Napoleon's army, who camped in Safed in 1799. The soldiers are said to have searched the area for the treasures. The first Jewish traveler to mention Ein Kahal was Rabbi David de Beit Hillel, who described his visit to the Holy Land in 1824 thus: "Some two hours after you leave Safed for Tiberias, you reach Ein al-Kahal, a spring with excellent water. It is near a very high cliff that is as straight as a wall from bottom to top. According to tradition, some of the holy treasures from the Second Temple are hidden in this mountain."

But where exactly are they hidden? At the very top of the cliff above Ein Sela is an arched recess that looks like a closed gate – a prime site for buried treasure. The tradition of Ein Kahal is also perpetuated through the name of the village of Kahal, which is located in the vicinity.

The marked path continues from Ein Sela to a dirt road that makes a good pickup point since it is passable for any vehicle. Those who came in one car can return by foot to Akhbara.

Another option is to continue for three kilometers beyond Ein Sela to the Parod-Amiad Highway (Highway 85) and enjoy the spectacular view of the Sea of Galilee and the Golan Heights along the way. In that case, the pickup point is at the sign to Nahal Amud on the highway.

Route 11:
Between Two Galilees

Nahal Amud is not just the only riverbed in Israel that runs north to south. It's also the only one that passes from the woods of the Upper Galilee to the jujube savannahs of the Lower Galilee.

Route length: 18 km.
Difficulty: Good hikers.
Start point: Parking lot of Safed's military cemetery.
Access: Safed.
End point: Approach road to Kibbutz Hukok.
Duration: 10 hours.
Admission fees: None.
Opening hours: None.
Remarks: Shorter routes: 1. End at Ein Koves – 8 hours. 2. End at the Parod-Amiad Highway (Route 85) – 7 hours if you start at the cemetery or 5 hours if you start at Ein Koves.
Equipment: Make sure to bring plenty of drinking water.
Pickup point for cars: End of route.
Map: Upper Galilee Hiking and Trail Map (No. 2).

| jan | feb | mar | apr | may | jun | jul | aug | sep | oct | nov | dec |

Early in the morning, we parked the car above Safed's military cemetery, taking advantage of the fact that a concrete staircase leads straight down from there to the city's old cemetery.

For hundreds of years, numerous tombstones have accumulated in the old cemetery. Some of them are quite dilapidated, but the tombstones of well-known people are painted either white or eye-catching shades of blue. Among those buried here are the famous kabbalists of Safed, the most prominent among them being Ha'ari, Rabbi Yitzhak Luria. There is nearly always someone praying beside their graves, hoping that the souls of the holy men will help the prayers reach the right ears.

Opposite is the beautiful scenery of the large, green Mt. Meron. Nahal Meron, which flows into Nahal Amud, looks like a slight wrinkle in the slope of the mountain. We could clearly see the abandoned British police station on its southern bank. It was built during the Arab uprisings of 1936-39 in order to protect the pumping station that brought Safed the water of the spring of Ein Yakim, which emanates from Nahal Meron. The prominent silhouette of Mt. Mitzpe Hayamim juts out from over the western bank of the riverbed.

We walked down the path between the graves to the lower plaza of the cemetery, where we came upon two fig trees whose branches were adorned with plastic bags and pieces of cloth waving in the wind – a clear sign that this was a sacred place. "Life exists thanks to the prayer of those who dwell in the dust," reads a sign at the spot, attributing the saying to the Zohar, the mystical tractate studied by many kabalists. We checked as thoroughly as we could. There is no such passage, but it is nice that someone bothered to convey to us a bit of the spirit of Rabbi Shimon Bar Yochai, who relates his kabbalistic vision in the Zohar.

The riverbed of Nahal Sechvi, via which we were to descend to Nahal Amud, was now very close, a bit north of the cemetery (to the right). But the new highway leading up to Safed blocked our way. We had no choice but to turn left (south) at the lower gate of the cemetery.

Beside a faded yellow building, we encountered the first blue trail marker. Here we turned right and crossed the highway below. Then we made another right turn (north) and walked parallel to the highway. We passed a grove, which also had its share of graves of holy men. Further on, two lovely funeral cypress trees, whose branches grow horizontally, signaled the descent to Nahal Sechvi.

The name of this riverbed (Riverbed of the Rooster) is based on its Arabic name, Wadi el-Jaj. The rooster's haunting cry is very compatible with the kabbalistic spirit of Safed.

We visited in spring, a delightful time to be in this area. Green carpets of Egyptian honesty grew among the Atlantic pistachio trees, together with tall columns of yellow asphodels and many other flowers. Amid all of this opulence, we nearly didn't notice the old paving stones that cover a segment of the riverbed.

The paving of Nahal Sechvi probably began in the fifteenth century, when Safed became a center for the production of high-quality woolen fabrics, which were

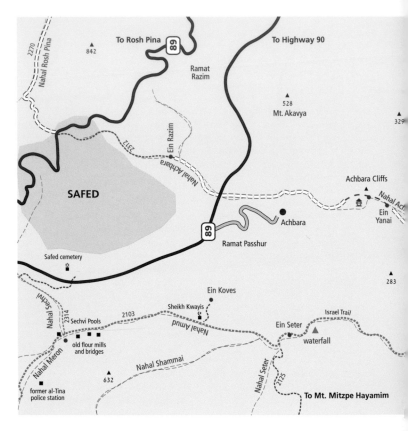

exported to customers all over Europe. The expertise in this field was brought to Safed by Jews who had been expelled from Spain and Portugal; they had first settled in Salonika and Adrianople, where they learned the trade.

Rabbi David de Rossi, who visited Safed in 1535, wrote: "Many Jews are arriving all the time and the clothing [textile] business is growing every day... and every man and woman who works in wool at any trade will earn a good living."

What do the textiles of Safed have to do with the paving stones in Nahal Sechvi? The answer lies in the fact that in order to turn the woven wool into felt, the wool

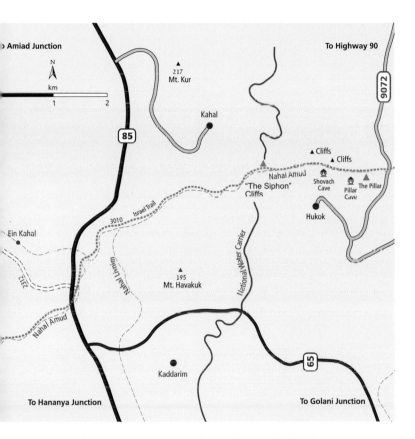

must be beaten repeatedly, until the threads are very tight. This process, which is known as fulling, shrinks the fabric to half its size.

In ancient times, a wooden club was used or the fabric was immersed in water and trampled on – a rather arduous process. In the twelfth century, a mechani-

cal fulling mill, driven by water power, was invented in Europe. Spanish Jews brought the new technology, which they called batan, to Safed.

The mechanical fulling mill changed the system of producing woolen fabrics. The industry moved from tiny workshops in large cities to rural areas with an abundance of flowing water; Safed's citizens utilized the water of nearby Nahal Amud. (The Arabic name of one of the structures in upper Nahal Amud, not far from the spring of Ein Po'em, is Tahunat el-Batan, a clear indication that at a certain stage in its life it functioned as a fulling mill.)

Textile merchants invested in the construction of fulling mills and it may have been they who paved Nahal Sechvi, which offered the shortest route to the Sechvi pools in Nahal Amud.

The shallow Sechvi pools, which contain water all year round, create a charming little corner of the riverbed. Large plane trees are reflected in the clear water, and there are also fig trees, an abandoned flour mill, and a cave. Few hikers can resist the urge to take a little break here.

We began to walk down Nahal Amud, following the black markers and the Israel Trail's blue, white and orange markers. During rainy winters, the riverbed turns into a rushing stream. We occasionally passed an abandoned flour mill. It can be assumed that the structures close to Safed served at some point as fulling mills. We also passed ancient arched bridges, which offered further evidence of the flourishing industry that once existed.

In 1576, the Ottoman authorities ordered the exile of 1,000 Safed families to Cyprus, an act that wiped out most of the city's textile industry. Jews continued to work in the industry on a small scale until the end of the seventeenth century, and the fulling mills were subsequently converted into flour mills.

Further down the riverbed, we no longer saw any mills. We were now in a purely natural setting. Interspersed with the trees of the Mediterranean wood were hedges of prickly pears and remains of olive and almond trees. A riverbank forest of huge oriental plane trees accompanied us all along the way.

After about an hour and a half of walking, we saw a blue trail to our left leading up to the spring of Ein Koves, a half-kilometer walk. The Hebrew name Ein Koves echoes the name of Sheikh Kwayis ("the good sheikh"), whose tomb lies on the side of the trail.

From Mt. Meron's slopes to the Sea of Galilee, Nahal Amud overcomes a height differential of about 1,200 meters in the course of only 25 kilometers, and so we knew it was only a matter of time until we came to a canyon with waterfalls. And sure enough, not far from the hidden spring of Ein Seter, we saw a long, narrow canyon, in which water cascades down mightily in winter.

The trail circumvents the canyon from the right and then leads back down to the riverbed. Here the trail shifts to the northern bank, but we continued along the riverbed for another 150 meters, in order to see the lovely curtain of water on the left side of the spring. The spring bursts out of a crack in the rock about 20 meters above the riverbed.

We returned to the trail and moved over to the eastern bank of the riverbed. We could see the water of Ein Seter flowing from the edge of a little olive orchard. The trail circumvents the continuation of the canyon from about 70 meters above it, offering a breathtaking view of green wooded slopes, the flowing canyon, and

Eastern Golden-Drop.

Nahal Amud.

the waterfall splashing into a large pool.

At the edge of the canyon, the trail returns to the riverbed, whose banks are now round shoulders instead of rugged cliffs. The woods thinned out as we descended. The plane trees were fighting an all-out war with the jujubes for control of the riverbed, but the increasingly warm climate and the dwindling of the water were giving the jujubes the upper hand.

This segment of the route features impressive populations of connate Alexanders (*Smyrnium connatum*, or *morit keluta* in Hebrew). It is one of the most beautiful wild plants in Israel because of the sheath at the base of each flower's stem that broadens into a cuplike shield; this plant has even been cultivated for ornamental purposes. It grows to about a meter in height and usually springs up between piles of rocks.

The Israel Trail leaves Nahal Amud for a moment and turns left on a dirt road that crosses the Parod-Amiad Highway (Route 85). There is a barrier against vehicular traffic, but a gate is open to pedestrians. The trail returns to Nahal Amud at its meeting point with Nahal Akhbara.

From here on, we walked along a dirt road used by herdsmen who graze their cattle in the area. For about 4 kilometers, the channel digs its way between erect limestone cliffs. Vultures nest on these cliffs, though a recent survey by the Bird-watching Center revealed that their numbers have diminished.

The National Water Carrier crosses the riverbed of Nahal Amud at this point; a network of pipes descends from the northern cliffs and then ascends the southern slope camouflaged in concrete.

About 20,000 years ago, the erosion that created Nahal Amud began to accelerate, leaving several caves suspended on the cliff. In 1925, they were the scene of the first prehistoric research in the Land of Israel, when British archaeologist Francis Turville-Petre excavated there. In one of the caves, he discovered the forehead bones of what became known as Galilee Man, who was estimated to be over 230,000 years old.

We soon reached the pillar (*amud*) that gave the riverbed its name — a column of rock about 30 meters in height, which remained in the area after the rocks around it were swept away.

In the 1960s, in the adjacent cave, Japanese archaeologists discovered a complete human skeleton from the Early Stone Age. Scientists were divided as to whether the skeleton was from a Neanderthal society or an "advanced" Neanderthal society.

Researchers from the Hebrew University of Jerusalem, Tel Aviv University, and the Institute for the Study of Human Origins (at the time in Berkeley, California) believe the question was resolved in 1992 when their excavations in the cave unearthed the skeleton of a 10-month-old infant whose skull fragments convinced them that a Neanderthal society had dwelled in Nahal Amud.

There is no dispute as to the identity of the car that waited for us beside the approach road to Kibbutz Hukuk: It was definitely a Neanderthal vehicle. Nevertheless, it brought us home safe and sound, after a great day of hiking.

Route 12:
Montfort Castle in a New Light

A few "minor" changes have made a world of difference in a traditional Western Galilee hike that includes the riverbed of Nahal Keziv, the spring of Ein Tamir, and Montfort Castle. Follow the ERETZ staff on 10 kilometers of the new route.

Route length: 10 km.
Difficulty: Moderate.
Start point: Approach to Montfort Castle.
Access: Drive from Mi'ilya toward Hila, pass Hila, and continue on the good dirt road (marked in red) that leads to Montfort Castle. After about 600 meters, having passed a turnoff onto a black trail (left) and a blue dirt road (left), you'll come to "our" black trail (on the right, 60 meters after a square area surrounded by a low concrete wall).
End point: Approach to Montfort Castle.
Duration: 5-6 hours.
Admission fees: None.
Opening hours: None.
Equipment: Regular.
Remarks: Any vehicle can be parked beside the beginning of the trail. The route is a ring route, taking you back to the starting point.
Pickup point for cars: End of route.
Map: Upper Galilee Hiking and Trail Map (No. 2).

jan feb mar apr may jun jul aug sep oct nov dec

Every time a new edition of a hiking and trail map comes out, I approach it with mixed feelings. On one hand, I look forward to seeing additional trails that open up fresh hiking possibilities. On the other, I'm afraid I might discover that trails I happily hiked upon for many years have been sacrificed on the altar of development.

As I studied the latest Upper Galilee Hiking and Trail Map, I noticed a change in the route of the black-marked trail that leads down to Keren Bartot and Ein Tamir. "The houses of Hila have expanded westward," Dani Gaspar, coordinator of the Israel Trails Committee, explained apologetically. "A new neighborhood has been built that covers the top of the trail. A new trail has been created to circumvent the urban encroachment."

But this wasn't the only change. Many hikers have been shocked to learn that the INPA has shaven away the forest of oaks that enveloped Montfort Castle.

I decided to take a 10-kilometer hike along the trail in order to formulate my own impressions of the changes. Gaspar accompanied me.

We started walking down the black trail from its beginning. On our right was a fence that ran along the perimeter of an agricultural field. The woods on the left eventually gave way to fruit trees, among them a lone Syrian pear tree.

Some say that at the beginning of summer, just when the tree's nearly spherical pears, which can grow to 4 centimeters in diameter, have ripened, you can chew the fruit and even swallow it, but the flavor is nothing to write home about.

The trail then leads down to the shallow upper segment of the riverbed of Nahal Bartot. A lovely forest grows in the gorge. Since it is in a spot that faces north and is therefore less exposed to the sun, it is the home of true laurels, which need more humid conditions. But most striking are the Eastern strawberry trees, whose red branches glow among the green trees. In summer, the red bark peels off and each tree becomes a work of art.

The trail crosses Nahal Bartot and soon reaches a junction with a blue trail. We took the blue trail to the left, adding another kilometer and a half of walking on Keren Bartot — a mountain horn that rises about 200 meters above a large bend in Nahal Keziv. The scenery is gorgeous.

At first, the blue trail runs above the riverbed of Nahal Bartot, where several little olive trees grow among the rocks. A short distance down the horn, Montfort Castle comes into view, on the horn of the mountain between Nahal Bartot and Nahal Keziv — hence Montfort's local Arabic name, Qala'at Qurein (Castle of the Little Horn). Without the trees that used to loom over it, the castle looked strange and even a little poignant. But when we got used to it, we had to confess that Montfort is now much more impressive.

The trail continues to wind along the periphery of the ridge to a bend in Nahal Keziv between Mount Ziv and the Nakar Shoulder. The landscape is a combination of a deep valley and rocky, wooded slopes. In the first two weeks of May, there's a bonus at the bend: the blooming of Madonna lilies (*Lilium candidum*, or *shoshan tzahur* — white lily — in Hebrew). After that, the lilies are replaced by the tall

Montfort Castle.

stalks of the rough-leaved michauxia (*Michauxia campanuloides*, or *mishoya pa'amonit* in Hebrew), which have strange-looking white flowers.

The Keren Bartot trail curves around the Bartot Horn and returns to the black trail. Turn left on the black trail and follow it down to Nahal Keziv. The black trail then leads down the riverbed, but we made a quick detour to the spring of Ein Tamir, which is located about 300 meters up the riverbed (to the east). On the way, we encountered a tempting pool that is a nice place to take a dip.

The spring of Ein Tamir flows out of a cleft in the rock in a clear stream that runs through an expanse of gleaming limestone. Unfortunately, the smooth surface has become a magnet for graffiti. The plastic bags and candy wrappers, forgotten socks, and leftover food strewn around the area are equally infuriating.

Further down the river are some pools shaded by plane trees. At the junction of the black trail leading to Moshav Goren, a group of large trash bins placed there with good intentions by the INPA have become a magnet for garbage. Somebody has to explain to the INPA that setting up garbage bins is not enough – someone has to empty them every now and then.

From the garbage bins, the trail turns into a wide dirt road, accompanied by numerous Syrian maple trees. This segment of the riverbed is dry in summer up to Ein Matzor, a spring whose water emerges below the ruins of a two-story stone building and dam on the southern bank, at the foot of Montfort Castle. The building and the dam date back to the Crusader period.

Archaeologists who explored the site determined that the dam created a lake whose water was used for irrigation. The building initially served as a flour mill, but a more elegant upper floor was later added, and apparently the building was then used to house pilgrims and guests.

At the junction with the red trail, follow it to the left up to the castle. Montfort Castle, which rises 180 meters above Nahal Keziv, a Crusader castle surrounded by dense woods amid the cliffs of Nahal Keziv, is a beautiful combination of nature and antiquities.

Excavations conducted at the site in 1926 by a team from New York's Metropolitan Museum of Art uncovered the remains of buildings, coins, and other objects from the Roman and Byzantine periods. Some of the stones of the donjon, the massive inner tower that is the castle's largest and tallest structure, may have been part of a Roman citadel that stood here. The stones of the castle were hewn in Horvat Nahat, about 200 meters up the trail ascending from the castle.

In the twelfth century, there was a much smaller castle in this area, meant to defend the estates of the local feudal lords; its remains lie under the old town center of Mi'ilya. In 1220, Hermann von Salza, head of the Teutonic knights, purchased a large tract of land in the Western Galilee, encompassing Montfort. The knights called the place Starkenburg (Strong Mountain), a German translation of the French Crusader name Montfort.

In 1226, the knights began building one of the most beautiful Crusader castles in the Land of Israel. It is not clear why they built it in this location, which lacked any special strategic value. It may have been meant to serve as a defense against the local residents, who were not particularly fond of the Teutonic knights.

Pope Gregory IX, calling for donations for the citadel's construction, said, "It is located on the border of the idolaters and therefore its construction will bring much benefit to Christians in those areas, since it restrains the Saracens and gives believers safe freedom from the usual troubles." The pope promised donors partial release from religious penalties that had been imposed upon them for their trespasses.

The Teutonic knights may also have chosen this location to keep their command headquarters far away from the eyes of the other orders, which were mostly French and were suspicious of the Germans.

In 1266, at the beginning of Mameluke sultan Baybars's drive to conquer the Galilee, one of his commanders tried to take Montfort and failed. Five years later, the sultan himself stood opposite the castle walls. The siege began on June 8, 1271, and the outer fortifications were conquered three days later. The sultan promised a large sum for each stone plucked out of the wall.

The fighting was fierce. Eventually, the castle's defenders laid down their arms, after it was agreed that they would leave as free men but without their possessions and weapons. They moved to Acre, managing to take with them the castle's archive and treasures, which were subsequently transferred to Venice and then to the Teutonic fortress in Marienburg, Poland. (They remain there to this day.) Montfort Castle was never inhabited again.

Now that the trees have been removed, the castle is visible even from a distance and it is easy to distinguish the three lines

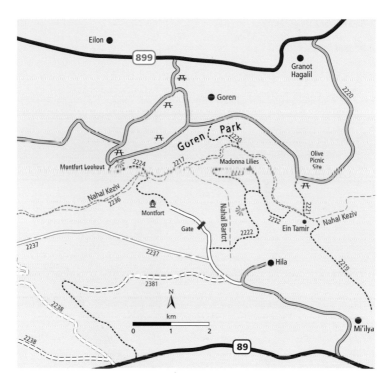

of fortifications. The internal wall has been exposed, including its gate tower and opening for pouring boiling liquids on invaders. The ceremonial hall is also very impressive. The large cisterns and clay pipes that collected water from the roofs of the castle can now be seen as well.

Follow the red trail through the castle and up to the outer wall on the northern side. Several courses of the wall's huge stones are still in place. The trail passes through the moat, which borders the castle on the east. Some 50 meters further on, it passes through a rock crevice, about a meter wide, with steep, 8-meter-high walls. The crevice appears to have been widened for use as an external moat.

The red trail will lead us back to the place where we parked the car. Before getting in to the car, take a glance back at the landscapes of the Sulam Ridge, which forms Israel's northern border, the Galilee coastal plain, and the sea – a wonderful backdrop for a castle.

Route 13:
From Yodfat to Tamra

Go up to Tell Yodfat, climb to Mt. Atzmon, descend to Nahal Avlayim and its springs, walk up to Kuakab abu el-Hija, and go down the lovely rocky riverbed of Nahal Kabul. Sounds long? A little, but it's not too bad. A great hike for good walkers.

Route length: 14 km.
Difficulty: For good walkers.
Start point: Parking lot in Tell Yodfat, access from the road to Moshav Yodfat. About 400 meters from Yodfat Junction a brown sign directs you southward to a dirt road (green). Drive about 1 km to a road marked in red, turn left, and drive about 1 km to the parking lot. The roads are rocky, but navigable.
Access: Road to Moshav Yodfat.
End point: The Tamra quarry, access from Route 70, from the northern entrance to Tamra (follow the signs). Park in front of quarry gate.
Duration: 7 hours.
Admission fees: None.
Opening hours: None.
Equipment: Regular.
Remarks: Members of Moshav Yodfat don't want hikers to walk through it and asked the Israel Trails Committee to remove the trail from it to Tell Yodfat.
Pickup point for cars: End of route.
Map: Upper Galilee Hiking and Trail Map (No. 2) and Lower Galilee Hiking and Trail Map (No. 3).

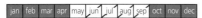

jan | feb | mar | apr | may | jun | jul | aug | sep | oct | nov | dec

There will probably be hikers who will raise an eyebrow at the faded sign indicating no less than three possible trails to hike in Tell Yodfat. After all, it's only one little hill. But still, you have to respect this round hill. In this spot, which rose on the stage of history for the first time in the writings of Josephus (*Wars of the Jews, 3, 7-8*), the first battle took place in the Great Jewish Revolt against the Romans. The Romans besieged Yodfat for 47 days, wrote Josephus, commander of the revolt in the Galilee, who led this very battle. The outcome for the Jews was not good.

From the sign until the end of the hike, you'll walk along a trail marked in blue. The trail goes up the northern slope of the hill beside several carob trees and reaches the ruins of the walls of Yodfat, some of them from the Hasmonean period and some of them apparently built in preparation for the revolt. On the tell's northern side, excavators found the ruins of a siege embankment.

The trail passes through the western part of the tell, beside water holes and caves. The water holes were the only source of water for the inhabitants of Yodfat.

Afterwards, the blue trail descends to the deep ravine of Nahal Yodfat. A bit ahead of you, further along the wall, excavators found a segment of a wall containing an opening of a vertical pier hewn in the rock. At a depth of 1.5 meters, it could be closed with a door. From the opening, a tunnel led to three underground chambers arranged in two floors. This hideaway also was built in preparation for the revolt.

The trail crosses Nahal Yodfat, passes through two openings in cattle fences, and climbs up a slope inside a grove that is not particularly thick, in which broad-leaved phillyrea, Kermes oak, lentisk, and dwarf chicory grow. They are accompanied by shrubs of prickly burnet and spiny broom. The best time to see it is in spring, when everything is in bloom. The sun's-eye tulips are in great abundance.

The trail first climbs along a little ravine that descends to Nahal Yodfat. Then you reach a dirt road, which you turn right onto, and after about 200 meters you turn left on another dirt road. The blue path soon descends to the left from the dirt road and climbs steeply to the top of Mt. Atzmon (547 m), which offers one of the most breathtaking views in the Galilee. From here, you can see the area that is between the Golan in the east and the Mediterranean Sea in the west, and between the mountains of Nazareth and Mt. Tabor in the south and to the mountains of the Upper Galilee in the north.

Even Mt. Atzmon played a role in the revolt against the Romans. In 66 CE, riots, rooted in disputes between Samaritans, pagans, and Jews, broke out in the area, which was part of the Roman province of Syria at the time. The riots led to the military campaign led by Castius Gallus, the Roman governor of Syria. The campaign ended with a resounding defeat of the Romans by the fighters of Shimon Bar Giora atop Beit Horon. Following this defeat, the Jews declared the Great Revolt.

When Gallus passed through the Galilee, Zippori opened its gates to him. At the same time, the rebels from the villages in the area raced to Mt. Atzmon. Though they managed to claim the lives of some of the Romans, they weren't a match for the

Roman army. In this battle, Josephus reports, more than 2,000 Jews were killed.

The trail then descends from the top of Mt. Atzmon southward to a dirt road. Walk west (right). After about 700 meters, the trail leaves the road and leads down to the springs of Nahal Avlayim. The riverbed has this name because it passes beside the village of Iblin, the location of Avlayim of Talmudic times. There are three springs in the riverbed and your trail leads down to the middle one, Ein el-Wasat; next to it is Ein el-Kaziza. These springs flow year round; their water collects in shallow pools. The third spring, Ein a-Tahta, is dry in summer.

The trail goes up the riverbed and reaches a broad valley containing wheat fields and a grove of ancient olive trees, one of the largest and most impressive in the Galilee. The trees are so elderly that some of the trunks are twisted and their owner fills them with stones in order to stabilize them. Here the trail climbs gently through young vineyards to a building with two domes – the grave of Sheikh Abu el-Hija – surrounded by the village cemetery. The stone building is fortified from the outside with strips of concrete that mar its appearance. The residents left behind several Kermes oak trees, which have grown a little more than the average. The building contains two rooms. The first, closest to the entrance, is used for prayer and gatherings. In the interior room, there are two tombstones.

Local traditions relate that the grave is the burial place of Sheikh Mohammed Bachri, an officer in Saladin's army who took part in the battle that was waged against the Crusaders at the Horns of Hittin (1187). In the adjacent village, Kaukab Abu el-Hija, there

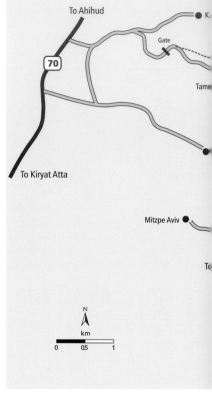

are four graves of sheikhs. The name Kaukab apparently retains the name of an ancient Jewish settlement by the name of Cochav or Cochba. An archaeological survey conducted at the site revealed potsherds that attest to a settlement that existed from the Iron Age (eleventh century BCE) until the Byzantine period (fifth century CE).

You can take a lunch break on the grass

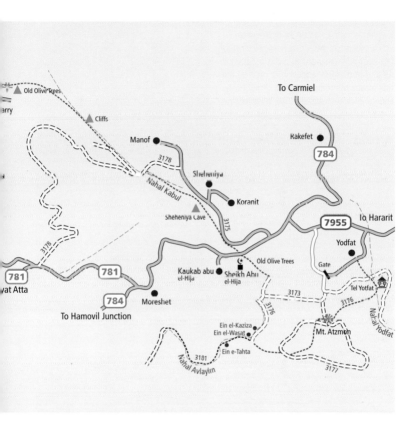

outside the cemetery, in the shade of the trees. Fans of Oriental cooking can go about 300 meters west to the gas station, where there is also a restaurant that serves food that is rather mediocre but edible.

The trail crosses Route 784 (be careful) and continues through a woods along a dirt road. The trail then leaves the dirt road and continues parallel to the access road of the communal settlement of Sheheniya. The trail leads to the cave of Sheheniya, located several meters to the left of the trail. The sign announces that entry to the cave is not permitted, since it is inhabited by a rare species of bats and entry to the cave is liable to endanger their existence, especially in winter, when they are hibernating.

A "transparent" trail marking (a marking

with two white stripes that invites hikers to go off the main route to an interesting site) leads to the cave's opening. The cave is located at the bottom of a *dolina* (a small karstic hollow), which absorbs the water that drains into it from the surrounding area. The *dolina* is a lovely corner where hikers can rest in the shade of large trees.

In 1992, the bones of Yisrael ben Zeev were found in the Sheheniya Cave. He was born in Yesud Hama'ala in 1905 and worked as a guard, preventing Bedouin in the area from taking hold of lands that had been purchased by the Jewish National Fund. However, in 1938, the Bedouin murdered him and threw his body into the cave. His body was found only 52 years later.

The blue trail reaches a dirt road marked in black. Here you turn left. After about 250 meters, turn right on a dirt road marked again in blue. Next to the cattle gate, the path goes off the dirt road and enters a shallow ravine that becomes deeper. This is the channel of Nahal Kabul. The riverbed's high banks are very rocky and beautiful. They form large, steep cliffs, full of crevices. Here and there you see new agricultural plots, at the expense of the undergrowth.

Nahal Kabul descends to the village of Kabul, but before the trail reaches the village, it turns left and climbs up the left bank of the riverbed. A large, beautiful terrace containing old olive trees overlooks the houses of Kabul.

The trail ends on a road inside the Tamra quarry. The hike comes to an end here, too. Now you only need to go down the road to the right to reach the gate of the quarry. If it is closed, ask the guard in the adjacent building to open the gate for you.

Syrian Cornflower.

An old olive tree.

Cemetery of Kaukab Abu el-Hija.

Hikers at the foot of Mt. Atzmon.

Yodfat.

Route 14:
The Road to Tabor

This two-day hike across the Lower Galilee begins at Beit Keshet, continues up Mount Tabor, and ends in the Jordan Valley.

Route length: 26 km.
Difficulty: Good hikers.
Start point: Entrance to Kibbutz Beit Keshet.
Access: Route 65.
End point: Kilometer marker 399 on Route 90. (1 kilometer south of Kibbutz Gesher.)
Duration: Six hours from Beit Keshet to Gazit Junction. Nine hours from Gazit Junction to the Jordan Valley Road (Route 90).
Opening hours: None.
Equipment: Regular.
Remarks: Security House of Beit Keshet: Museum and Film. Fax: (04) 662-9028.
Church of the Annunciation (Franciscan): Open Sundays to Fridays, 8 a.m. to noon and 2 p.m. to 5 p.m. Closed on Saturday.
Accommodations: Mount Tabor Hotel: Gazit Junction. This hotel is the most convenient for hikers since it is located right alongside the trail.
Tabor View Hotel: A friendly guest house with 120 rooms located at the entrance to Kibbutz Mizra.
Pickup point for cars: End of route.
Map: Lower Galilee Hiking and Trail Map (No. 3).

jan | feb | mar | apr | may | jun | jul | aug | sep | oct | nov | dec

Start this two-day walk at the grand old oak tree at the entrance to Kibbutz Beit Keshet. When it comes to estimating the age of a tree, even normally level-headed individuals can display a tendency towards exaggeration, particularly when faced with a specimen towering dozens of meters into the air. Local folklore, for instance, relates that the Crusaders tied their horses to the majestic oaks of Horshat Tal in the Upper Galilee. According to other stories, the sycamore trees along the coastal plain, a species whose lack of tree rings makes it difficult to date, sprung up naturally thousands of years ago.

Similarly, the impressive Mount Tabor oak standing just west of Route 65 by the access road to Kibbutz Beit Keshet is the subject of many legends and stories. The sign by the tree states that it has been here since the time of Napoleon Bonaparte, who passed by this site in the Lower Galilee after failing to conquer Acre.

Napoleon had come here to extricate part of his army from a Muslim force marching from Damascus that had overwhelmed the French brigades near the village of Fula (site of present-day Afula). Napoleon eventually won a slim victory. Being a good public relations man, he designated the fight as the "Battle of Tabor" — knowing that the reference to this mountain associated with the New Testament account of Jesus' transfiguration would resonate in the Christian world more effectively than the "Battle of Fula." And indeed, the battle is noted on a Parisian monument memorializing the great battles of France.

Back here in the Holy Land, meanwhile, the battlefield itself became known to local Arabs as Marach al-Frange, which means the "French campground."

The sign alongside the Mount Tabor oak also notes that this very same tree appears in a picture from the Napoleonic era, a drawing of the adjacent Khan al-Tujjar, or the merchants' khan, as it was known. Indeed, the remains of Khan al-Tujjar lie just on the other side of the modern-day Route 65, which runs north-south between Kfar Tabor and Golani Junction right along an ancient caravan route that once linked Damascus with Egypt and Sinai. The khan was built by Sinan Pasha, who was the governor of Damascus around 1588, and was used as a way station along the caravan route. A few hundred meters to the north of the oak tree lie the ruins of yet another khan, it is known as "Kalat Souk al-Khan," and was built in the Mameluke period to guard the way station and the caravan route. As the names suggest, this was a big open-air market that flourished here even in the early twentieth century, when many a trader rested under the shade of this oak tree.

In addition to its commercial draw, however, the tree has a special emotional significance to the Bedouin of the a-Sheih tribe, who have lived in this area ever since migrating here in the eighteenth century from a region of what is now Turkey. It is alongside this tree that an a-Sbeih clan sheikh, Ahmed Shihab, is buried. A highway bandit, he gained a reputation of being a Bedouin Robin Hood who shared his stolen goods with the poor. Ahmed Shihab was strong and daring enough to extort protection money from the adjacent

Jewish village, Kfar Tabor, which was founded in the late nineteenth century. In the end, the Ottoman rulers of the period decided to put a stop to his activities. In 1906, he was killed in an ambush.

This tree is connected to yet another story, from the pre-state era. The Paicovitch family from Kfar Tabor had a wheat field in the area. Local Bedouin often tried to plunder the fields. When Yigal Paicovitch reached bar mitzvah age, his father gave him a pistol and ordered him to go down to the wheat field at sunset to stand guard.

"Don't shoot," the boy's father warned him. "Shots can kill and will only drag us into a blood feud."

The boy went off on his mission, hid near the tree, and began his watch. Not much time had passed when two armed Bedouin arrived, and started to reap the wheat. Young Yigal loaded his pistol, yelled at them, and shot into the air. At the same moment, he heard his father behind him curse the intruders and then give chase. The father had indeed sent his son on a dangerous mission – but he followed him all the way. Yigal, who went on to become one of the founders and commanders of the Palmach, later changed his last name to Allon (which means "oak" in Hebrew) in honor of the story.

From the oak tree, walk several hundred meters west along the road that runs to Kibbutz Beit Keshet, before heading south, or left, along a broad dirt road towards a squat, white, concrete building sitting in the fields. The building has six rooms in a row on the first floor, and one large room on the second floor, along with a watch-

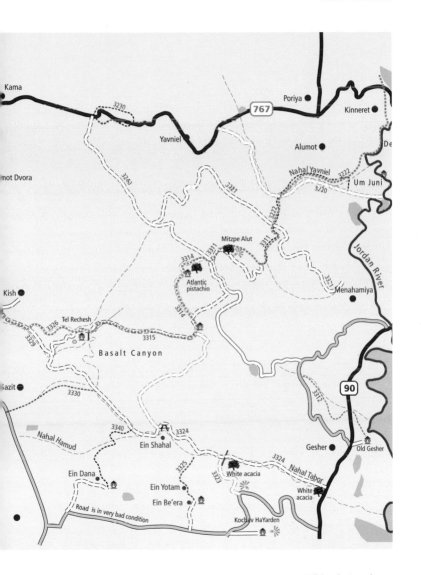

tower. This was the site where 50 young men and women first established Kibbutz Beit Keshet on August 15, 1944, the most veteran of the Palmach settlements.

At that time, the kibbutz extended over only four acres of land, surrounded by a fence. Five watch stations, connected by trenches, protected the small land holding. Kibbutz members lived in shacks and tents, while the concrete structure was used as a shelter in times of tension.

The trails that pass alongside Beit Keshet have been favored passageways from the Sea of Galilee to the Beit She'an Valley and the Mediterranean coastal region since time immemorial. Flint tools collected in the area give testimony to the fact that today's Route 65 was even a migration path for prehistoric man. Similarly, early Jewish settlers saw it as a strategic area. Beit Keshet, in particular, was established as an effort to beef up the Jewish presence around the Kadourie Agricultural School, located just to the south, and one of several lone Jewish outposts in the area at the time.

Natan Fiat, the famous director of Kadourie, requested that a kibbutz be established alongside the school in order to enhance its security. And indeed the area suffered from security problems and isolation. There were only 30 families in nearby Kfar Tabor and Ilaniya [to the north] was home to a similar number. In contrast, the two Arab villages in the area had some 5,000 residents.

It was also intended that the new kibbutz would help prevent Bedouin encroachment into a forest that stood nearby and had been acquired previously by the Palestine Jewish Colonization Association (PICA), which had been founded by Baron Edmond de Rothschild. The forest included approximately 75 acres of native oak woods, which is the present-day Beit Keshet Forest.

In the period of Israel's War of Independence, Beit Keshet was a frontline outpost that suffered many casualties. In March 1948, a group of youths from Beit Keshet were out on a tour of a nearby hilltop, known as Shihab Hill, when they were ambushed by Bedouin. Seven people were killed, including Eli Ben Zvi, the son of Yitzhak Ben Zvi, who later became Israel's second president.

Two weeks before the declaration of the state, and the invasion of the armies from neighboring Arab states, the members of Beit Keshet staged a surprise attack on the a-Sbeih tribe on Shihab hill; many were killed and the rest fled. But meanwhile, another 700 Arabs came to rescue the Bedouins and another 17 members of the kibbutz were killed. Twenty-seven men thus lost their lives on Shihab Hill. As a result, the kibbutz members decided that they would put their permanent settlement on the same site. The center of this "permanent settlement" was the concrete structure known as a "security house," which is today a small museum.

Continue west along the kibbutz access road, turning off just before the entrance to a small paved road that heads south into the JNF's new "Scenic Road" through Beit Keshet Forest. The road, which soon becomes a smooth dirt track suitable for cars, passes through a wonderful forest of Mount Tabor oaks. Of all of the trees grow-

White acacia woods in Nahal Tabor.

ing wild in Israel, the Mount Tabor oak most lends itself to the sense of a true "forest," creating a wood of large, well-spaced trees interspersed with shrubs and bushes, and carpeted with fallen leaves.

After walking for a while along this wide dirt track, and following the scenic road as it heads westward, you will meet up with the Israel Trail, which heads southward toward Mount Tabor. The trail continues onto the edges of Shibli below Mount Tabor, the present-day home of one branch of the a-Sbeih tribe that stayed in Israel after 1948. In the 1960s, many of the young men from the village began to volunteer to serve in the Israeli army, where they gained a reputation as outstanding trackers and fighters.

Along with the Bedouin village, two other Arab towns ring the lower slopes of the Tabor: Dabbouriyeh and Um al-Einam. The upper two-thirds of the mountain is occupied by church institutions, including a Greek Orthodox church and the Catholic Monastery of the Transfiguration. Much of the land around the summit is also designated as a national park.

Turn westward, or right, along the road that encircles Mount Tabor and walk along it for about 500 meters to the "Tabor Terminal," a large parking lot for tourist buses that sits alongside a bathroom and a small, shuttered food kiosk.

The ascent to Mount Tabor is fairly steep, if not difficult or dangerous. The mountain is isolated from the other nearby ridges of the Nazareth range. It rises some 350 meters from the flat farm fields around it.

The footpath leading to the top winds its way through Mount Tabor oaks and pines. Higher up on the dolomite cliffs, where the red-tiled Greek Orthodox monastery roof is visible through the trees, you will find more common oaks. The views from here are stunning. You can see Safed in the Galilee, and Mount Hermon. Closer by is Beit Keshet Forest, the kibbutz, and the old white security house standing alone in a field. Along with the present-day monastery, ruins from various ancient periods dot the summit. Among them are military reinforcements from the Roman era, when the Jewish commander Yosef Ben Matityahu spent time here during his preparations for the 67 CE Jewish revolt against the Romans. He was captured at nearby Yodfat. In Roman custody, he changed his name to Josephus Flavius and began a new career as a historian chronicling the era of the revolt.

Clearly, however, most of the ruins on the mount are connected to the Christian traditions that identify this hill as the place where the transfiguration of Jesus took place. The event is described in the New Testament:

"After six days Jesus took Peter, James, and John with him and led them up a high mountain, where they were all alone. There he was transfigured before them. His clothes became dazzling white, whiter than anyone in the world could bleach them. And there appeared before them Elijah and Moses, who were talking with Jesus. Peter said to Jesus, 'Rabbi, it is good for us to be here. Let us put up three shelters, one for you, one for Moses, and one for Elijah.' Then a cloud appeared and enveloped them, and a voice came from the cloud: 'This is my son, whom I love. Listen to him!'" (Mark 9: 2-7)

Nowhere is it explicitly written that this event took place on Mount Tabor. But related New Testament texts make it relatively clear that it occurred somewhere in the Galilee. And so, by the end of the fourth century, when the first church was built here, Mount Tabor had become associated with the transfiguration. Along with the Greek Orthodox church, a Catholic monastery was built here between 1919 and 1924. Elements of the ancient church were integrated into the modern structure.

It is also worth noting that the first conference on *yediat ha'aretz*, or Israel lore, was held atop this mount on October 1, 1948. The conference took place while Arab forces continued to fight the army of the new Jewish state not far away. In the evening, conference participants sang and danced around a campfire, and on the following day, a Sabbath, they hiked down to Harod Spring (Ma'ayan Harod) in the Beit She'an Valley.

Circle the southern face of the mountaintop, along the path that hugs the monastery wall. On the eastern edge of the summit, descend through oak woods, still following the Israel Trail, which overlaps with a blue-marked trail.

On your left are stunning views of the Lower Galilee, the Horns of Hittin, the Sea of Galilee, and Mount Hermon. The trail ends up at the easternmost edge of the village of Shibli. Passing through an olive orchard, walk east toward Gazit Junction where Routes 65 and 7276 intersect. Here, the Israel Trail runs right by the Mount Tabor Hotel, where the dedicated hiker can take a break and resume his walk the very next day. Alternatively, try the bed-and-breakfast lodgings at Kibbutz Kfar Tabor

Autumn mandrake.

Mount Tabor.

just up Route 65 or the Tabor View Hotel alongside Kibbutz Mizra, at the junction of Routes 73 and 60 north of Afula.

From the Mount Tabor Hotel, the Israel Trail descends into the Nahal Tabor Nature Reserve via Route 7276 to Kfar Kish. The Nahal Tabor riverbed, which drains into the Jordan Valley, is best known to hikers for its "Basalt Canyon," where wildflowers and blossoming almond trees bejewel the walls of the high rock cliffs in the spring.

Tel Rechesh is a large man-made hill that actually lies right between two riverbed channels. The Hebrew name for the site was derived from the Arabic name – Tel al-Muchrachash. Serious excavations have never been undertaken here so it is difficult to ascertain just what ancient settlements might be identified with this area.

There are those, however, who see this site as the ancient city of Anharet, which is mentioned in the Book of Joshua as one of the cities of the tribe of Issachar, which controlled the Nahal Tabor area.

From Tel Reches, we finally descended into the Basalt Canyon. Hikers flock to this site in the spring to enjoy the incredible blossoming of the blue lupin. At the end of January, when we took this hike, the white buds of the almond trees were also in the height of bloom.

During the winter, the canyon, like the rest of the riverbed, is full of water. We walked along one channel through a narrow passageway in the canyon carved from the basalt. At the heart of this passage, below a little waterfall, is the Red Pool, named after the red earth around the area, which was created from the slabs of basalt. Toward the exit from the canyon,

the riverbed widens and reconnects to a red jeep trail, a little less trafficked, that heads southeast toward Kochav Hayarden, known to the Crusaders as Belvoir.

Those who wish can leave the riverbed here via a blue-marked footpath that heads south along Nahal Be'era. The trail goes past three springs as well as the ruins of the village of Be'era. The first spring has no name. The second is Ein Yotam.

Further up the stream, alongside the ruins of the village, is Ein Be'era, the biggest of the springs. The site is graced by picnic tables and plum trees. Some historians identify the village of Be'era with the biblical settlement of Be'er to which Yotam Ben Gideon fled after cursing the Canaanite residents of Nablus for betraying the legacy of his father (Judg. 9:21).

We, however, recommend continuing on the red-marked trail east along the Nahal Tabor riverbed. The last four kilometers of the trail through the valley is a real pleasure in winter and spring. The trail is wide, but closed to jeeps and thus particularly pleasant for walking. It is lined with white acacia trees all the way to its end point at Route 90, the Jordan Valley Road. The white acacia is a rare tree in this country, growing only in a few places. It doesn't replicate from seeds, but rather from shoots put out by roots. That's the reason that this acacia is usually found in dense clumps of bushes. The valley is also a good place to spot deer. In fact, some 1,300 deer roam in the wild in the lower and eastern Galilee. Even in winter, it's very warm here on a sunny day. But you can cool off by wading occasionally in the stream, whose waters flow here all year round.

Mount Tabor.

Mount Tabor Oak.

Persian cyclamen.

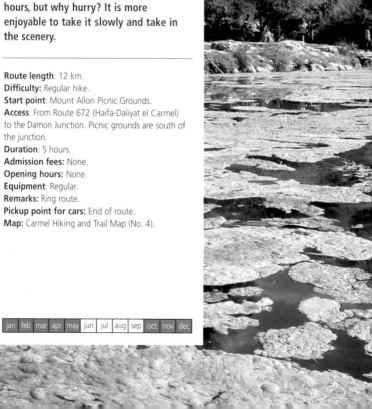

Route 15:
To the Allon Valley and Nahal Kelah

Nimble hikers probably could complete the hike along this ring route in five hours, but why hurry? It is more enjoyable to take it slowly and take in the scenery.

Route length: 12 km.
Difficulty: Regular hike.
Start point: Mount Allon Picnic Grounds.
Access: From Route 672 (Haifa-Daliyat el Carmel) to the Damon Junction. Picnic grounds are south of the junction.
Duration: 5 hours.
Admission fees: None.
Opening hours: None.
Equipment: Regular.
Remarks: Ring route.
Pickup point for cars: End of route.
Map: Carmel Hiking and Trail Map (No. 4).

jan feb mar apr may jun jul aug sep oct nov dec

Start the walk at the Mount Allon picnic grounds, right next to the Damon Junction. The picnic grounds are a little difficult to locate, especially since there is no sign indicating that they are there. Once at the picnic grounds, make your way along the small, narrow path that is barely a trail and that begins just south of the picnic grounds. It leads to the dirt road that descends into the riverbed of Nahal Allon. According to the map, there is a trail marked in blue along the riverbed, but the markings are difficult to find.

Nahal Allon is a typical Carmel riverbed. That is to say, between the Kermes oaks (*allon matsui* in Hebrew and *Quercus calliprinos* in Latin), cyclamen, and anemone, are old tires and the rusting skeletons of cars that someone dragged to the riverbed to abandon. A pine forest planted by the Jewish National Fund and a natural Mediterranean forest cover Nahal Allon's slopes. Tangled bushes of chained genista (*retema kotzanit* in Hebrew and *Genista fasselata* in Latin) grow on the chalk slope. This plant is common throughout the entire Middle East, but in Israel grows only on the Carmel mountain range for reasons that no botanist has yet been able to explain.

Tree branches and even some trunks block the path, but after a few minutes' walk, the going becomes easier and begins to resemble a leisurely stroll through nature. The Nahal Allon riverbed becomes deeper, providing some pampered true laurel trees (*Laurus nobilis* in Latin and *ar atzil* in Hebrew) with the shade and moisture that they need to flourish. The trail also passes a black pipe that someone installed to illegally funnel water from the riverbed. A large

pine tree that was completely uprooted lies on its side in the middle of the path ahead.

Nahal Allon descends into a small, lovely valley surrounded by mountains called Allon Valley (Biqa't Allon). On the side of the valley is Mount Arkan, rising to a height of 480 meters above sea level. On its slopes, though hidden from our view, are the houses of Givat Wolfson, which were originally built as summer homes in 1950. Today they serve as permanent residences.

The Allon Valley is approximately 1.5 km long and 0.5 km wide. In the past, almost the entire valley was utilized as farmland, but due to the low financial returns on farming in Israel today, most of the Allon Valley is now covered with olive groves. Cows graze there in winter, giving it a European look.

The Allon Valley was formed by the Nahal Oren river, which runs through it and washed away the tufa rocks that once covered this region. Some of these soft porous rocks can still be seen on the valley's edges.

A dirt road with green trail markings runs through the valley. Turn southward (left) onto this road, pass a small grove with about a dozen cedar trees and then leave the green-marked trail, turning right at a trail junction on the spot where a small boulevard of large Kermes oaks and a large Cyprus oak (*allon hatola* in Hebrew and *Quercus boissieri* in Latin) grow next to Nahal Oren. From here, follow the black-marked trail and the Israel Trail in order to begin the ascent to Mount Shokef. The path is very steep, but not very long, and so the climb only takes about 15 minutes. A large Cyprus pine grows next to the trail.

The trail leads to a wide path that runs

between a mixture of planted trees and natural undergrowth. From here, follow the black-marked trail and the Israel Trail. We are on Mount Shokef, which at 497 meters above sea level is among the highest of the mountains in the Carmel. Despite its promising name, which means observation mount, all that we can see is a narrow strip that includes the buildings of Kibbutz Beit Oren and Haifa and a tiny bit of the Mediterranean Sea.

The trail leads to the Rakit Ruins. The site's Hebrew name sounds similar to its Arabic one: Rukitiya. The ruins are mainly the remains of a Byzantine-era settlement. There is a beautiful burial cave that was carved into the stone. It includes a courtyard and an arched entryway. Three rosettes are carved on the facade of the entranceway and the remains of an inscription in Greek can be seen above it. Towards the end of the Ottoman period, there was a small Druze village here. It was destroyed in 1840, in response to the Druze rebellion against Egyptian ruler Ibrahim Pasha.

At the Rakit Ruins, leave the Israel Trail and follow the red trail markings that lead downward and across a wide path. This trail continues through a grove alongside the Nahal Rakit riverbed, with the riverbed on the left and a wide dirt road on the right. Continue to descend along this path until you reach the Agam (Lake) picnic grounds, which is one of the largest picnic grounds in the Carmel region and is located by Nahal Oren, the riverbed that drains the Allon Valley.

There's no chance of getting lost at the Agam picnic grounds and no need to search for trail markers leading to it. Just head toward the right on the river's slope until you see the red trail markers again. The trail crosses the paved road that leads to Givat Wolfson and then reaches a small dam. In winter and spring, the waters from the Oren Spring create a real stream here. The dam traps some of the water, creating a nice little lake, behind which grows a tall palm tree.

Follow the trail over the dam and then ascend the northern bank of the river, making your way through a thicket of oleander (*harduf hanehalim* in Hebrew and *Nerium oleander* in Latin). Part of this path is paved, a sign of its importance in the past. The path leads to the remains of a flourmill. This is the sign for you to leave Nahal Oren and ascend the slope on the left, following the green trail markers.

The path leads to a large open area at the foot of a big hill known as Hirbet Shalala near a sharp curve of the road that ascends to Beit Oren. Before reaching the road, about 50 meters before the parking area, turn left by the big carob tree, where an opening has been cut in the rock. The ancient residents of Hirbet Shalala, built the stepped path there that leads to the Oren Spring, from which they drew water.

A team of archaeologists from Bar-Ilan University, led by Prof. Shimon Dar and Yigal Ben Efraim, discovered the remains of settlements from the Roman period and the Middle Ages at the site. Though the team did not conduct extensive excavations and more work is needed, the initial findings led Dar to hypothesize that Hirbet Shalala is the site of the city of Carmel that first-century Roman historian Pliny mentioned in his writings. The city of Carmel is also mentioned in the Middle Ages as the town that

Nahal Oren.

Allon Valley.

a woman named Miriam fled from so that she would not be forced to marry someone against her will.

Much later, in the early 1920s, Shukri Mansur, a translator for the German consulate, acquired about a thousand acres of land in the Hirbet Shalala area. Mansur rehabilitated the Ottoman farm on top of the hill and planted an orchard in Nahal Oren. He also planted a vegetable garden.

In the early 1930s, Josef Levy arrived in the area. A man with vision, Levy established a development company which acquired 1,500 acres of the land at Shalala. The area was called the Carmel Forest due to the many tall pine trees in the area.

At the time, the area was considered to be a great distance from Haifa, which has since expanded. The distance deterred people from settling there. The investors, most of whom were of German origin, decided to pay a group of laborers to work the land, build roads, and bring life to the area. The workers were promised that when people began settling in the area, they would receive land on which to build their homes. In October 1935, 15 workers were allocated to the site. They used camels to transport their equipment to the area by the Oren Spring. They set up a tent camp, which they named Mishmar Hacarmel, and began paving roads, cultivating the orchard, and growing vegetables.

When the Arab Revolt began in April 1936, the workers relocated to the farm at Hirbet Shalala. They fortified the site, strengthening the outer walls. They were joined by reinforcements – Jews serving in the British police force and settlers from other communities. Despite their efforts, repeated Arab attacks and ambushes claimed 15 lives. The group was so upset by this that it gave the Jewish National Fund the rights to 325 acres of the land at Hirbet Shalala. On October 1, 1939, the JNF arranged for the first members of Kibbutz Beit Oren to settle at the farm at Hirbet Shalala. A few members of the Mishmar Hacarmel group still resided there. The tension between the two groups was so great that a year later the members left for another site, where the kibbutz is located today.

Today Hirbet Shalala is a picnic area called the Mishmar Hacarmel farm. The site is maintained by the Israel Nature and Parks Authority.

The dream of creating the settlement of Carmel Forest was shelved, though a few signs of the dream can still be seen in this area. The area is covered with a network of roads and the remains of the early settlers' orchards can be seen at Nahal Oren. In addition to Givat Wolfson, the Carmel Forest Spa is located in this area today. The luxurious spa was originally built in the 1960s as a convalescence home for German Jews.

Continue to the parking area and then follow the black-marked trail that leads out of the parking area and runs alongside the curving highway. Pass a round stone that is all that remains of the many olive presses once located here. This stone was part of the equipment that crushed olives in order to produce oil. The path leads past a cave and into a shady forest where the rocky ground is slippery.

When the path reaches a small valley, leave the black-marked trail, turn left, and walk for about 30 meters to an impressive ancient quarry. Many signs of the ancient

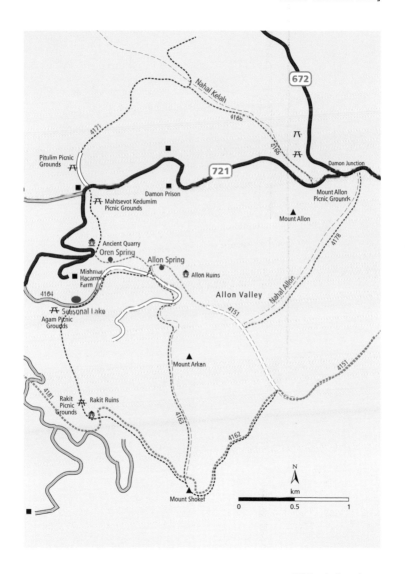

quarry can still be seen today. This quarry apparently was the source of the stones that were used to build Hirbet Shalala in the Byzantine period.

Return to the black-marked trail and follow it up the slope to the Mahtsevot Kedumim (Ancient Quarry) picnic grounds. The large picnic area is built along a dirt road that leads directly to the junction of Kibbutz Beit Oren, where the Cat Ballou horse ranch and restaurant are located. Cross the road carefully here and continue on the dirt road with red trail markings (4171), making your way past the Pitulim picnic grounds, another of the many picnic grounds in the Carmel.

The path then descends to the Nahal Kelah riverbed and its beautiful cliffs. The high stalks of Madonna lily (*shoshan tsahor* in Hebrew and *Lilium candidum* in Latin) can be seen growing between the cliffs; its large white flowers perfume the air in May.

The dirt road leads to Nahal Kelah and its stone bridge. The bridge and the dirt road are the remains of British attempts to fortify the Carmel against a German attack during World War II. The Germans never came, but the bridge is still here.

The bridge is a sign to turn right at the ascent of Nahal Kelah and follow the path with blue trail markings (4166). Before doing so, however, continue about 100 meters up the road in order to view one of the most famous sights in the Carmel: An interesting rock that rises to the impressive height of 30 meters. Erosion has taken its toll on the lower part, forming an area that is shaded by the upper part of the rock.

From here, return to the bridge and continue on toward the grand finale of the hike.

Nahal Kelah is one of the most beautiful riverbeds in the Carmel. The riverbed is completely shaded by Mediterranean forest. The shade makes it possible for moss to grow here, covering the rocks with a lovely green carpet.

Walk on the slope of the riverbed, climbing over small rockfalls and enjoying the shade provided by laurestine (*Viburnum tinus* in Latin and *moran hahoresh* in Hebrew) and true laurels, which have joined the Kermes oaks. The beginning of the riverbed is a shallow valley that contains abandoned terraces on which oaks grow to impressive heights.

Continue along the path to the road and cross it to reach the Mount Allon picnic grounds, where we began the hike.

Nahal Kelah.

Route 16:
To Love Bay and Beyond

A hike along the seashore from
Dor-Habonim Beach to Caesarea.

Route length: 17 km.

Difficulty: Moderate.

Start point: Dor-Habonim Nature Reserve. Entry via
the access road to Moshav Habonim (Route 4,
kilometer marker 183). Instead of entering the
moshav, turn onto the dirt road leading to the beach
(it's signposted), carefully cross the railroad tracks,
and leave your car in the reserve parking lot.

Fee: Summer – NIS 20 per car, NIS 60 per bus.

Access: From Route 4.

End point: Aqueduct Beach in Caesarea, or further,
in the Caesarea National Park.

Duration:7-8 hours, including dips in the sea.

Admission fees: None.

Opening hours: None.

Equipment: Shoes or sandals for wading and plenty
of drinking water. (Fill-up point: Tantura Beach.)

Remarks: Crossing Nahal Taninim at its mouth is
permitted only in summer, when the current in the
riverbed is slow. It is absolutely forbidden to cross the
channel after a rainfall.

Pickup point for cars: Aqueduct Beach in
Caesarea.

Map: Carmel Hiking and Trail Map (No. 4).

| jan | feb | mar | apr | may | jun | jul | aug | sep | oct | nov | dec |

To reach the beginning of the trail at Dor-Habonim Beach, turn off on the access road to Moshav Habonim, take the bridge over the Haifa-Tel Aviv highway, drive a few meters to the left, and turn right on the dirt road to the beach. At a makeshift gate, you will be asked to pay a parking fee of NIS 20. Continue to the large parking lot, beside a concrete wall.

Beside the wall is a box containing free leaflets from the Israel Nature and Parks Authority (INPA) introducing visitors to the reserve. A trail marked in red leads up from the parking lot to the top of the ridge. North of this point stretches the reserve's northern cove. Camping in the cove is permitted.

Right below the parking lot is Shell Cove, a little inlet on the *kurkar* (calcareous sandstone) ridge covered with a carpet of shells that are thousands of years old and have only recently washed up on the shore. (Hikers are asked to leave the shells in place.) This is only one of the reserve's many picturesque coves, which were created by the waves that nibble at the ridge. Dor-Habonim Beach is, in fact, perhaps the most beautiful beach in Israel.

Walk southward on the ridge. In May, the scallop-leaved sea lavender will be in full bloom. The headed thyme blooms in summer. In the southern part of the reserve, where the red trail leads away from the shore and a green trail branches off from it, is "The Hill of Blossoms" – named for the many tulips that bloom there in March.

The green trail returns to the parking lot, the end of the short route through the reserve. For this hike, follow the red trail to Love Bay, a no-man's-land between the nature reserve and Tel Dor National Park.

Further south you come upon Tel Dor.

This ancient site, one of the most important cities in the ancient Land of Israel, situated in a lovely part of the coast, has not been developed for visitors.

The town apparently dates back to the Middle Canaanite period (eighteenth century BCE). Excavations were first conducted there in 1923-24, by a British expedition led by Prof. John Garstang (founding director of the Department of Antiquities in the British Mandate of Palestine). In 1950, parts of a Roman theater were exposed, and since the 1980s, an expedition from the Hebrew University of Jerusalem, led by Prof. Ephraim Stern, has been working there.

In Hellenistic and Roman sources, Dor is said to be located between the tip of the Carmel and Caesarea; Roman geographer Eusebius places it 9 miles north of Caesarea. To make matters even more certain, excavators at the site have uncovered a lead weight from the Hellenistic period inscribed with the name Dor.

North of the tell, south of Love Bay, are the ruins of a seaside Roman theater. On the edge of the bay are walls that are the remains of warehouses and a dock.

On the southwestern side of the tell is its main cove, which was used as an anchorage. South of the cove are the remains of a temple from the Hellenistic period – apparently the famous temple of Poseidon, the god of the sea. Dor's streets were built in this period; only a few have been excavated.

South of the temple rises the acropolis, containing remains of a Crusader citadel; it affords a clear view of Dor's southern cove, which features the remains of a port from the Late Canaanite period. Parts of Dor's massive fortifications have been uncovered and the remains of a Byzantine church have been found east of the town.

Equally exciting finds were discovered off the coast of Dor, whose beach is still called Tantura, for the Arab village that stood here. "The king of the beach" is Kurt Raveh, a Dutchman who came to Israel as a volunteer during the Yom Kippur War in 1973 and stayed. Raveh has taken part in excavations at Tel Dor, served as an inspector for the Israel Antiquities Authority, established the Glassworks Museum in Nahsholim, and fished treasures out of the sea. Today he is director of the Aqua Dora Diving Club, which is also the base for Haifa University's underwater archaeological research.

In Dor Bay and its surrounding area, 17 boats have been discovered so far, from periods ranging from the Canaanite era to the twentieth century. In ancient times, boats entered Dor's harbor from the south, via an opening in the marine platform. They attempted to move northward, the water in the port flowed southward, and the boats crashed into the shoals and sank.

A ton and a half of old coins have been found on Tantura Beach, as well as many pottery vessels. Cannons and other weapons have also turned up here – some of the gear of 12,000 French soldiers who lightened their load during Napoleon's infamous retreat from Acre.

South of Dor, the ridge and deep coves are gone. There are no trail markings, but you can't get lost. Simply walk southward along the beach, right between the sea and the fishponds.

Nahal Taninim's outlet into the sea is one of the most romantic places along the beach

Caesarea Aqueduct.

to watch the sunset. The mouth of Nahal Taninim has to be waded across. In summer the water is knee-deep. Do not attempt to cross the river before the month of May as the current can be lethal. The Ottoman Turks built an arched bridge here for German Emperor Wilhelm II, who passed through in 1898 on his way from Haifa to Jerusalem. Its remains are clearly visible.

South of the riverbed, on Tel Taninim, we come upon the Israel Trail, which leads down to that point from the Carmel Range and continues southward to Caesarea. This is the only place in the country where the Israel Trail runs near the seacoast. Tel Taninim contains the remains of Krokodilopolis (City of Crocodiles), which flourished in Roman and Byzantine times. In the Crusader period, the town was known as Turris Salinarum (Saltworks Tower), perhaps because salt was produced in the area. The hike ends with a 3-kilometer beach hike. The trail continues parallel to the Roman aqueducts along the beach. The time to arrive at the end of the hike, at Caesarea beach, is towards evening, as the sea swallows up the sun and shrubs of evening primrose light up with their large yellow flowers.

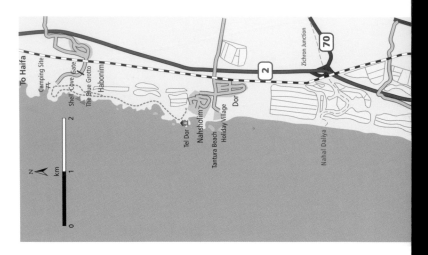

Dor-Habonim Nature Reserve.

Tantura Beach.

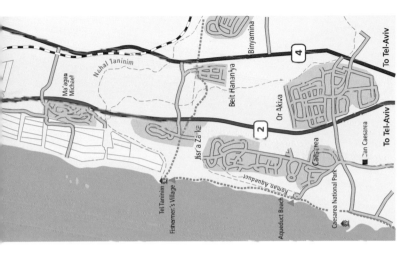

Evening primrose.

The Blue Grotto.

Route 17:
From Port to Port

The ports of Tel Aviv and Jaffa are connected by a seven-kilometer promenade. It's a fun place for a hike in good weather.

Route length: 7 km.
Difficulty: Easy.
Start point: Kedumim Square, Jaffa.
Access: From Razif Ha'aliya Hasheniya Street.
End point: Tel Aviv Port.
Duration: 2-4 hours, depending on the distractions.
Admission fees: Admission charge to the Etzel Museum.
Opening hours: Etzel Museum: Open Sun.-Thurs. 8:30 a.m. to 3:00 p.m. Friday, 8:30 a.m. to noon, Tel. (03) 517-7180.
Equipment: Hat and walking shoes.
Remarks: None.
Pickup point for cars: End of route.
Map: Map of Tel Aviv.

| jan | feb | mar | apr | may | jun | jul | aug | sep | oct | nov | dec |

The entrance to the Jaffa Port is somewhat hidden, but if you make your way from Kedumim Square in Old Jaffa toward the sea, you eventually reach the area where the streets are named for the signs of the zodiac. If you took Simon the Tanner Alley, turn right. If you took a more northern path, turn left. One way or the other, you will eventually discover a sign pointing toward the decorated gate beyond which lies the Jaffa Port.

Despite its international reputation and the oranges that are named after it, the Jaffa Port is not that impressive. The section of the limestone reef peeking out of the sea here is known as Andromeda's Rock, after the heroine from Greek mythology. The reef may create a safe harbor for those who are landward of it, but crossing the section of it hidden by the water poses a difficult and dangerous challenge for sailors.

The Ottoman Turks prevented the development of the port. Instead, large ships were forced to anchor outside the port and passengers and goods were ferried in on boats. The British built the breakwaters that can be seen from the port. Instead of struggling with the reef, they built the breakwaters to raise the water level above it, leaving only the northern edge above the water, just enough evidence for tour guides to retell the Andromeda myth over and over. A number of fishing vessels anchor in the small port, as well as boats that take tourists for short cruises along the Jaffa shoreline.

A stroll through the Jaffa Port quickly reveals that it is still waiting for redemption. Above the wharf are big old buildings from the Ottoman period, like the Greek monastery that has been here since the mid-seventeenth century. Here and there, you can see a pretty balcony, but the most dominant feature is neglect.

Exit the port through the decorated gate. On your right is the "Armenian Courtyard" (the Monastery of St. Nicholas). Today, about 60 Armenian families live in Jaffa and one of them traditionally held the keys to the building. The building was sold recently and a new housing complex is being constructed on the site that gained international fame during Napoleon's campaign in the Land of Israel (1799). It was where the French army quartered soldiers stricken by the plague. Some suspect that Napoleon ordered that the ill soldiers be poisoned, though there is absolutely no proof of that. The "Sea Mosque" (Jami al-Bahr) is next to the courtyard and the promenade begins just across from it.

This section of the promenade has been thoroughly rehabilitated. Around the first curve is Margaret Tayar's famous fish restaurant and just past that you can catch your first glimpse of the many cafes built to make the most of the promenade and the sea view. From here, it is only a stone's throw to Charles Clore Park. The Etzel Museum, 1947-1948 (Beit Gidi) is located in the park in a stone building – one of the prosperous homes of what was once the Arab neighborhood of Manshiya. The Etzel attacked Manshiya on April 25, 1948, cutting it off from Jaffa after five days of fighting. Some say that this attack was unnecessary since that same week the Haganah began Operation Hametz, in which all of Jaffa was conquered. In any case, the museum commemorates Etzel's activities during the War of Independence.

Bograshov Beach.

From the museum, you can see the steeple of the Abu Kabir Church, the neighborhood of Neve Tzedek, the Shalom Tower, and the great bloc of buildings that begins with the Dan Panorama Hotel and ends with the Hasan Beq Mosque. After continuing around the curve, stop for a moment to look southward at the beautiful peninsula of Old Jaffa jutting out into the sea.

The Hasan Beq Mosque and its minaret look out of place at the foot of the Dan Panorama Hotel and the towering office buildings. Hasan Beq, the ruthless military governor of Jaffa during World War I, built

the mosque from property he confiscated, claiming that it was needed for the war. The mosque and Manshiya comprised the border dividing Tel Aviv and Jaffa.

After passing the Dolphinarium, the promenade changes. The limestone cliffs of Jaffa end and the promenade truly runs along the sea. With beaches like these, it is hard to understand why anyone goes to the French Riviera. Every beach radiates the good life with its own cafés, colorful lounge chairs and parasols, golden sands, and blue water.

The promenade continues along the coast, from Jerusalem Beach to Atarim

Square. Slightly before the square, take a short detour to the park next to the Dan Tel Aviv that was built to honor the immigrants who defied British limits on Jewish immigration during the mandate period.

A word to the wise: There really is no reason to climb all the steps to Atarim Square; it is possible to walk along the lower part of the square, which passes by Gordon Pool.

The section of the promenade by the Hilton can also be bypassed by cutting through Independence Park, which is on a high cliff overlooking the beach. This is where the Muslims of Jaffa began to bury their dead during an outbreak of cholera in 1903. They selected this site because at the time it was far from the crowded city.

From the edge of the park, you can descend to Hof Metzitzim, or Peepers Beach. Just past it is the Tel Aviv Port, which has become one of the main entertainment spots in Tel Aviv. The port was dedicated in 1936 and operated until 1965, leaving behind an area that was recently converted into a popular entertainment center: old hangars have been turned into trendy cafes, restaurants, designer shops, and nightclubs, all connected by a huge wooden deck.

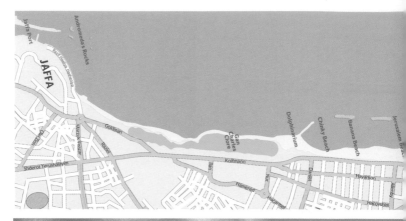

Jaffa Port.

Route 18:
The Jerusalem Trail

A new trail allows hikers to understand Jerusalem's geography and check out its historic sites from an unusual angle.

Route length: 4 km.
Difficulty: Easy.
Start point: Mount Zion Hotel.
Access: Hebron Road, Jerusalem.
End point: Park Zurim.
Duration: 3 hours.
Admission fees: None.
Opening hours: St. Onuphrius Monastery: Open to visitors Mon. to Fri., 9 a.m.-noon and 3 p.m.-6 p.m.
Equipment: Regular.
Remarks: None.
Pickup point for cars: End of route.
Map: Map of Jerusalem.

jan | feb | mar | apr | may | jun | jul | aug | sep | oct | nov | dec

Nobody, it seems, has a reasonable explanation for why the 950-kilometer-long Israel Trail, which extends from Kibbutz Dan to Eilat, does not pass through Jerusalem. The trail starts to climb toward the city, making its way along the Jerusalem Mountains, and then, just 5 kilometers before the city limits, it makes a U-turn and rushes back to the Coastal Plain. Like Richard the Lion Hearted, hikers on the Israel Trail can only gaze upon the houses of the eternal capital of the Jewish people from afar.

One excuse that is given is that the trail does not pass through cities, even though it cuts right through Netanya, running along its shorefront promenade from north to south. The Israel Trail also happens to pass through Tel Aviv, reaching the city along the Yarkon River. So the "no cities" explanation doesn't pass muster. Maybe the trail planners wanted to avoid it because of security and diplomatic considerations Jerusalem raises; it is unclear. Whatever the reason may be, hikers can now cross the entire country without entering its capital.

As a consequence, an innovative idea was raised by the "green" developers of Israel — the Jewish National Fund, the Israel Nature and Parks Authority, and the Society for the Protection of Nature in Israel. Their idea was to design a Jerusalem Trail that would connect the city to the Israel Trail as well as create a new way to see Jerusalem — on foot, via a circular trail. The idea of the Jerusalem Trail actually fit in well with the idea of creating a natural urban environment made up of parks and open spaces that are linked by hiking and walking trails in Jerusalem.

The result is the recently marked Jerusalem Trail, which leads from the spot where the Israel Trail makes a U-turn near Sataf (to the west of the city), climbs up to Ein Kerem, continues up to Yad Vashem and Mt. Herzl, extends from there to the area by the Knesset and Supreme Court, cuts through the garden suburbs of Rehavia and Talbiya, leads past the Old City to French Hill, and then runs down the riverbed of Nahal Sorek back to Sataf.

We decided to check out a 4-kilometer segment of this trail that offers a unique view of Jerusalem's historic sites. It runs along the Hinnom Valley at the foot of Mt. Zion, along the walls of the City of David, along the Kidron Valley and by the ancient tombs of the Mount of Olives, through Gethsemane, and, as a grand finale, up to the Gerald Halbert Observation Plaza overlooking the Judean Desert and the Dead Sea. It is a fascinating half-day walk that is full of surprises.

We began our hike just before the steps on Hebron Road leading down to the Jerusalem Cinematheque, where a blue path marker points to the right, indicating the trail that slowly descends into the Hinnom Valley.

The Hinnom Valley is mentioned in the Bible as the border between the tribes of Judah and Benjamin. In the First Temple period, a spot called Tofet in the valley was where the firstborn male children were sacrificed as burnt offerings to the God of the Ammonites — Moloch. King Josiah outlawed this practice, but the valley — whose Hebrew name, Gai Ben Hinnom, means the valley of the son of Hinnom — continued to be synonymous with hell and hellfire. Jeremiah prophesied that at the end of days Gai Ben Hinnom and the altars of Tofet standing in it would be called the Valley of Slaughter. Jeremiah's harsh words gave rise to the idea that the Hinnom Valley is actually Gehinom or Gehenna, the hell in which the wicked will be punished with fire after their death. According to the Talmud, "there are two palm trees standing in the Valley of Hinnom, and smoke comes up between them… this is the opening of Hell." The "Hell of Fire," as the valley became known, was also mentioned in the New Testament as the terrible place where the wicked will be judged.

The beautiful and peaceful valley through which the trail leads today has neither palm trees with smoke billowing out between them nor altars to pagan gods. Instead, as the path makes it way along the imposing cliff on the south side of the valley, it passes many caves and crevices in the rock face. Some of them are ancient burial caves, others are just natural fissures — but, for all those who know the history of the valley, they are a little eerie.

The slope toward the riverbed has terraces with olive trees growing along them, while opposite looms the bare, steep slope of Mt. Zion. "One of the first things we had to do in order to create the path and the park around it," says Menahem Fried, the Israel Nature and Parks Authority ranger in charge of the park, "was to remove tons of debris that had accumulated over the past 40 years." After the reunification of Jerusalem, in

1967, the Hinnom Valley became a favorite place for the illegal dumping of building debris. To return the park to its natural state, the debris had to be removed. In addition, barriers were erected to prevent trucks from entering the area and continuing this practice.

The center of the Hinnom Valley used to be the border between Israel and Jordan. The Jordanian and Israeli military outposts still stand, silently facing each other. A barrier of concrete dragon's teeth (concrete antitank wedges) stands guard in the valley, waiting to stop Israeli tanks if they ever dared to cut through the Hinnom Valley on the way to the Old City. The attack, when it finally erupted, came from the rear, with the Israeli tanks driving down the road and reaching the dragon's teeth from behind.

At the place where the path crosses the road, which descends from Abu Tor and Givat Hanania, stop for a moment, turn right, go up the road a bit, and turn right again along the track that leads to a blue metal gate. Push it open (it opens sideways) and enter one of the most fascinating and unknown places in Jerusalem: the Karaite cemetery.

The Karaite community in Jerusalem ceased to exist after Israel's War of Independence and the destruction of the Karaite synagogue in the Old City. The community had lived in Jerusalem since 750, when, according to Karaite tradition, the founder of the sect, Anan Ben David, settled in Jerusalem. The Karaites believe only in the laws written down in the Bible itself and not the oral tradition that developed after it. They are called Bnei Mikra, which is Hebrew for "sons of the Bible" and is the source of the Hebrew name of the sect: *karaim*. The Karaites, who in the Middle Ages had a larger community in Jerusalem than the "rabbinical" Jews, did not get along with the rabbinical Jews. This animosity is one of the reasons for the neglect of the cemetery.

The cemetery on the slopes of the Hinnom Valley is first mentioned in 1583 by Rabbi Moshe Mitrani (the Mabit), from Safed. "I, the Mabit, have been asked about the graves of the Zadokites called Karaites," he wrote. "They are considered Gentiles, so that priests (*cohanim*) are allowed to enter their cemeteries."

The text on the tombstones starts with the words *baruch hagozer* (Hebrew for blessed be he who determines fates) followed by the Karaite symbol of the open fingers, split two by two, like the sign of the priests. Then the text on the tomb continues with a long story in rhyming Hebrew verse about the man or woman who "looked miserable and died in the great war" or "who was a *zaddik* all her life" and so on. Most of the older tombstones that are still readable are from the first decade of the twentieth century and from the eve of World War I.

After exploring the cemetery, return to the path that continues down the valley. At the fork, bear left and then left again, and walk down the steps that probably date back to the Byzantine period. At the bottom of the steps, turn right and follow the path to the Greek monastery of St. Onuphrius. It is built over a labyrinth of rock-cut tombs that are full of the skulls and bones of medieval priests and pilgrims. The monastery is the traditional site of Haceldama, which comes from the Aramaic words *hakel dema* or the field of blood. This is the "fuller's field" that was bought with the 30 pieces of silver – the price of Judas' betrayal of Jesus. In Byzantine times, the many anchorites that inhabited the caves in the cliff around the monastery turned it into a place of atonement. The Crusaders built a church here and the cemetery beside it became a pilgrims' cemetery. The current building was constructed in 1874 and named after the Egyptian hermit St. Onuphrius.

The trail now follows the road to the intersection at the end of the valley. Turn left and follow the road up the Kidron Valley. A 100-meter walk will bring you to the southern end of the City of David – the site of the recently discovered Pool of Siloam. The pool, which was built in the first century BCE, was where the waters of the Spring of Gihon collected after flowing through Hezekiah's Tunnel. It was a famous gathering place during the Second Temple Period and was mentioned in many sources, including the New Testament, when Jesus sent a blind man to wash his eyes in the pool and be cured.

The path now follows the riverbed of Nahal Kidron. The village of Silwan is on the right and the City of David on the left. After passing the entrance to the Spring of Siloam, the path runs by the Second Temple period graves at the bottom of the Mount of Olives cemetery. The graves, known as the Grave of the Prophet Zechariah and the Pillar of Absalom, belonged to the wealthy priestly families of the Second Temple period.

Jerusalem Trail.

Hezekiah's Tunnel.

Hinnom Valley.

Rock climbing at Hinnom Valley.

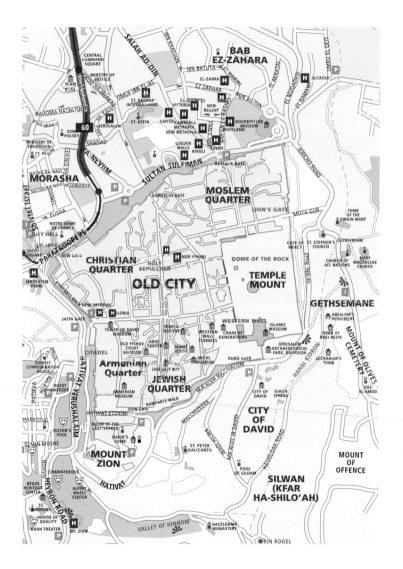

After passing the Pillar of Absalom, the path climbs up to the information booth on Jericho Road at the entrance to Gethsemane, which has many interesting sites and is worthy of an article of its own.

The path briefly joins the road that runs up the Mount of Olives, between the Church of All Nations and the Chapel of the Agony. Bear left at the fork in the road, and then turn left, following the blue trail markings, in order to reach the continuation of the path.

This part of the trail traverses one of the lesser-known corners of Jerusalem – the slopes of the Mount of Olives. As you walk alongside the ancient olive trees, the Valley of Jehoshaphet is below you and the walls of the Old City are on the other side of the valley. The vistas that open up between the olive trees highlight the Old City Walls, the Dome of the Rock, the Golden Gate or the Gate of Mercy, the Lion's Gate, and more.

After a few minutes' walk, you will reach the Orson Hyde Park, named after the Mormon leader who visited Jerusalem in the 1840s. The park was created as a gift to the City of Jerusalem following the founding of Brigham Young University. It is beautifully tended. Mohammed Yassin, the gardener, has been coming here daily to look after the park for 17 years. "Hardly anybody comes," he remarked, as we sipped black coffee under the old pine trees and enjoyed the view of the Old City. A path meanders through the park to the top of the slope, opening up different views of the Old City.

The Jerusalem Trail does not go through the park, but veers to the left at the gate and runs down the Valley of Jehoshaphat, through an assortment of ancient trees. The top of the valley has not been developed yet, since the debris on the left slope has to be carted away. The huge mountain of debris was removed from the vaults under the Temple Mount when a mosque was built, without a permit, in what is known as Solomon's Stables. The debris has to be sifted, excavated, and checked before it can be removed. The initial work done on it, in the nearby Emek Hazurim (Flint Valley), has shown the debris to be an archaeological gold mine.

Now follow the path to the road that leads up to A-Tur, cross the road and continue along the path (through the parking lot) into the Zurim Park on the other side. The path crosses the park, again studded with old olive trees, and then climbs up toward the Hebrew University of Jerusalem on Mt. Scopus, reaching the observation platform at the top. Don't stop here, but continue a little further on, across Martin Buber Street to the Gerald Halbert Park and Observation Plaza. The plaza looks out over the Judean Desert toward the Dead Sea.

This segment of the Jerusalem Trail has taken us from the cultivated Hinnom Valley, past the spring of Gihon – Jerusalem's ancient water source – and up the mountain overlooking the desert. This 4-kilometer hike makes the geography of Jerusalem – between the sown area and the desert, between the nomad and the farmer – easy to understand. The new Jerusalem Trail is a must for every lover of Jerusalem and all those who want to better understand the city.

Route 19:
Porcupines, Emperors, and the New Middle East

Beside the slopes descending from the Judean Mountains to the Ela Valley, an ancient road is hewn in the rock. Now marked and known as "the Emperor's Road," this route can be the highlight of a splendid spring hike, suitable for anyone ready to walk a bit.

Route length: 11 km.
Difficulty: Moderate.
Start point: Tzur Hadassah Junction (meeting point of Routes 375 and 386).
Access: From Jerusalem along Route 375.
End point: Tzur Hadassah-Ela Valley Road, parking lot at the foot of the olive press (Route 375, between kilometer markers 8 and 9).
Duration: 5-6 hours.
Admission fees: None.
Opening hours: None.
Equipment: Regular.
Remarks: None.
Pickup point for cars: End of route.
Map: Approaches to Jerusalem Hiking and Trail Map (No. 9).

| jan | feb | mar | apr | may | jun | jul | aug | sep | oct | nov | dec |

More than anything else, Tzur Hadassah Junction symbolizes the end of the age of innocence in Israel. The natural conditions are wonderful: mountain slopes covered with old agricultural terraces, the aroma of good soil mingled with the scent of pines, and clear air. Until recently, even the community of Tzur Hadassah had a pleasantly undefined character – not a kibbutz, moshav, village, or city, it was just a little place beside Mt. Kitron.

Don't bother to try to find Mt. Kitron today. It's now a neighborhood of Tzur Hadassah, with private houses coated with light-colored stone. Some 20,000 people are meant to live in Tzur Hadassah in houses like these in the future. Soon the houses and those of Beitar Ilit, situated on the next ridge, will be right next to each other.

Jerusalem's city hall is 14 kilometers from here, as the crow flies. Some day soon, municipal officials will start talking about demographic problems, pull out maps and statistics, and then claim that, in fact, Tzur Hadassah is an integral part of Jerusalem.

But on a nice spring day, what does all that have to do with a nice nature hike? The Israel Trail, marked with orange, blue, and white stripes, reaches this point on its way westward. This marking will accompany us throughout the hike. The telltale stripes can be found on the electrical poles at the junction. We turned on to the dirt road that enters a KKL-JNF grove, beginning the first segment of our hike before reaching the Emperor's Road.

At first, walk parallel to the road leading to Bar Giora. The trail soon descends to the left, down the upper tributaries of the riverbed of Nahal Zanoah, and passes beneath a massive high-tension line. Known as Line 400, it belongs to the days when people were talking about a New Middle East and the electricity flowing through it was meant to flow through Egypt and Jordan as well.

At the top of the slope to the right, the beautiful terraces of the abandoned village of Ilar al-Foka and a *makam* (a shrine to a Muslim holy man) with a white dome can be seen. In his guidebook to the Land of Israel, Zev Vilnay called the *makam* Sheikh Ahmed el-Hubani; nineteenth-century traveler Victor Guerin referred to the site as Sheikh Hubin.

Continue down the road without going up to the *makam*. When the path meets a paved road leading from Moshav Matta, turn right toward a large terrace and ascend to the antiquities site known as Horvat Darban. The walk among the terraces, covered with little shrubs of wild marjoram and other undergrowth, is a refreshing change. In winter, some of the trail markings disappear under the high grass, but it is easy to keep sight of the ancient stone wall that stands atop Horvat Darban and encloses an area containing almond trees.

Horvat Darban acquired its name when a porcupine (*darban* in Hebrew), digging itself a burrow in the southern slope of the ruins, exposed a potsherd bearing an imprint stating "for the king." An examination of it revealed it was from the time of King Hezekiah (705-701 BCE). Archaeologist Yohanan Aharoni subsequently dug at the site and found pottery from the Persian period (538-332 BCE).

The site abounds with caves hewn in the

Milestones along the Roman road.

rock and stunning views: Horvat Beit Itab, to the north, looks like a remnant of a fortified building; the moshavim Bar Giora and Ness Harim occupy the adjacent peaks; and below lie the houses of Moshav Matta.

The trail passes the walled area in Horvat Darban, meets up with a blue-marked trail, and descends westward toward Matta. The eucalyptus trees beyond the moshav mark the site of the spring of Ein Matta.

Until the trail reaches the spring, it runs past hewn openings in the rock, prickly pear hedges, and terraces laden with fruit trees. Blue lupins sprout here in abundance in January and bloom with lovely flowers in March. Numerous cyclamens grow on the last terrace, beside the road that runs along the periphery of the moshav.

After passing a palm tree nursery, the little eucalyptus grove is reached. A small brook flows nearby, and on its eastern side is a small man-made pond, with stalks of narrow-leaved reedmace growing in it.

The spring itself is situated a bit further up the riverbed. Horvat Tanor, beside the spring, contains such ruins as a large stone house with arched windows and walls that have survived to a height of about seven meters. Estimated to date to the Crusader period, it is thought to have served as a manor or perhaps a monastery.

Between the house and the spring is another little spring, Ein Tanor. Local legend has it that this was the site of Noah's stove (*tanor* in Hebrew). The stove, it is said, was submerged in the great flood. After the waters receded, the stove, tired of heating food, decided to produce water instead,

Emperor's Trail.

Reconstructed olive press.

which it does to this day. Guerin described this site as having orchards with trees so luxuriant that no ray of light could pass through their leaves.

The Israel Trail makes its way up the southern slope of Nahal Zanoah to Horvat Hanot (Khirbet el-Khan), situated in the shade of a forest where KKL-JNF has created a pleasant picnic site. The road beside Horvat Hanot leads up from the Ela Valley to Bar Giora (Route 375), following the route of an ancient thoroughfare. The ruins of a khan, or caravansary, in Horvat Hanot, attest to the ancient road's existence. The khan's walls survive, as well as a floor covered with sand that conceals a colorful mosaic from the Byzantine period; the sand protected it from vandals over the ages. Beside the khan is an ancient

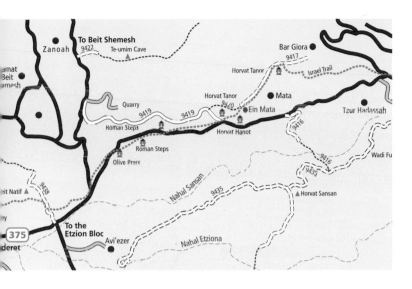

wine press, which has a simpler, white mosaic floor.

A large sign states that this is the beginning of the Emperor's Road, which is clearly delineated not only with the markings of the Israel Trail, but also with the local trail markings (white-red-white), KKL-JNF also has marked the trail with large rocks along the periphery.

Follow the trail through a lovely Mediterranean wood mixed with a sparse forest of pines. You will soon reach hewn steps in the rock. Archaeologists suggest that these steps were part of a Roman road from Ashkelon to Jerusalem, built in 130 CE in honor of the visit of Emperor Hadrian – hence the name Emperor's Road, given to it by a KKL-JNF employee.

The trail is narrow, pleasant, and meant for pedestrians, but those walking along it on a Saturday are liable to come upon cyclists looking for challenges. Walk down the steps to Nahal Hanativ. On reaching the road that runs through the riverbed, you will see a square underground cistern. Shaped similarly to Nabatean cisterns in the Negev, it is apparently from the Roman period. A round column supports its natural rock ceiling and the original plaster remains on a few walls.

Cross the riverbed via a small wooden bridge, and then pass five fragments of large, round columns, which probably served as milestones on the ancient road. A reconstruction of part of an old olive press stands nearby. Descend to the large plaza beside the Tzur Hadassah-Ela Valley Road, where the hike ends.

Route 20:
Stepping Out in the Yattir Forest

On the edge of the Judean Desert, in an area with limited rainfall, grows the largest forest in Israel – the Jewish National Fund forest of Yattir. The Israel Trail makes its way through the forest, which offers some surprises for hikers, including free accommodations and a beautiful Roman road.

Route length: 18 km.
Difficulty: Good hikers.
Start point: "Antenna Hill" to the west of Hurvat Yattir.
Access: The scenic western road of the Yattir forest is on the Beersheba-Hebron highway, about 2 km from the entrance to Kibbutz Keramim.
End point: The highway to the quarry and Drejat.
Duration: 7-8 hours.
Admission fees: None.
Opening hours: None.
Equipment: Regular.
Remarks: To arrange to stay at Mt. Amasa, contact Moran at Tel. (08) 955-5761.
Pickup point for cars: End of route.
Map: South Hebron Mountains Hiking and Trail Map (No. 12).

jan | feb | mar | apr | may | jun | jul | aug | sep | oct | nov | dec

If you haven't been to the Yattir forest recently, you are bound to find that the area has gone through many massive changes. If you take the scenic eastern road through the forest, you will soon find yourself at the separation fence, which cuts arbitrarily through the northern part of the road, near Nahal Eshtamoa. In order to overcome this new boundary, JNF rangers and the Israel Trail staff have decided to mark a new portion of the Israel Trail to make sure that the fence will not prevent hikers from making their way along the trail.

Because of the fence, our trip starts at the dirt road that begins at the Meitar forest and is marked in blue. The drive along the road is a great trip in itself — it is a kind of Israel forestry museum. The road passes through groves and clumps of trees that are not so common in the Land of Israel, like pistachio orchards and the eucalyptus torquata with its beautiful red flowers. Mesquite (*prosopis farcta* in Latin and *yanbot hasadeh* in Hebrew) is another interesting plant found here. To the Israeli farmer, this plant is a small bush that fills the fields and makes them difficult to plow. In North America, on the other hand, it grows into a tree. Some of the tree like plants were imported from America and planted in the Yattir forest on the edge of the desert, where they are doing very well. Picnic tables placed underneath the trees make this a favorite picnic site for families from the nearby community of Meitar.

The road crosses Nahal Eshtamoa and starts to wind its way through the region where the large village of Yatta is located. At the point where the road reaches the riverbed it also meets up with the separation fence, turning into a kind of military patrol road. As a result, the army filled the riverbed with rocks so that the track would not be washed away during flash floods. A layer of asphalt was poured over this so that even regular cars can now cross this major desert riverbed. However, it is doubtful that it will hold up against a serious flood.

Past the riverbed of Nahal Eshtamoa, parts of the scenic road have already been paved. The first turn to the right leads up a hill with a towering antenna perched on its summit. The Israel Trail passes at the foot of this hill — and this is the point to start the hike. From here, the hike follows the Israel Trail.

The path runs along the edge of a young forest along a wide dirt road with large stones along the margins that is reminiscent of an ancient road. Around us are the typical rolling hills of the desert fringe carpeted with low bushes that are covered with yellow flowers during the winter. This hike may be one of the last times that we can enjoy this view of the desert fringe — as we were checking out this route we received a hint of what is about to happen when we reached the paved road that leads to a big flat plot of land which used to be a Nahal encampment and will soon become a new settlement. Another new settlement is planned right next to it.

It is worthwhile to walk over to the edge of the large plateau where the new settlement will be built in order to take in the view. From here, we can see the separation fence, the settlements of Tene and Shima, and the industrial area of Yattir. Above them are the huge Arab villages of Dura and Yatta. The outskirts of another Arab village, Samoa, can also be seen. In the east, Mount Amasa peaks over the horizon. Beneath us is a low hill with the remains of some structures on it. This is Hurvat Yattir.

Hurvat Yattir is usually identified as the Levite city of Yattir, which also appears on the sixth-century Madeba map. In the Bible, it is mentioned as one of the cities of refuge, in which people who had killed someone by mistake could find refuge. Most of the remains that can be found here are from the Byzantine period and the early Arab period, including two churches, dwellings, cisterns, caves, graves, and wine presses. In the past, the tombs of two sheikhs stood on the site. One of them was Sheikh Attar, a local holy man whose name is reminiscent of the name of ancient Yattir.

From Hurvat Yattir, the trail descends along an unpaved road between pistachio orchards and a forest. At the clearing in which three date palms are planted and a few picnic tables are strewn, keep going straight by following the Israel Trail markings. Immediately after the clearing, the trail leaves the road and turns into a small ravine that leads through another pistachio orchard, along an ancient terrace built of large stones, and ascends the opposite slope of the ravine until it reaches the fence around the forester's house.

A little before the fence, a trail marked with two white stripes with no color in between them leads to the remains of an ancient quarry and a large water cistern.

The trail circumvents the forester's house to the right (west) and enters the house through its main gate. The forester's house was originally planned as a foresters' village – a place where the forest caretakers could live with their families. The building itself was built like a small fortress because at the time

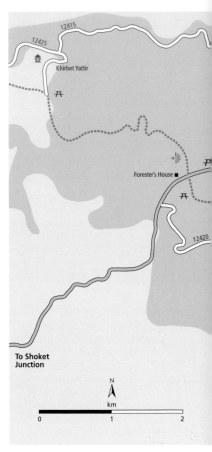

it was built (1965) Yattir was a border area and the fortress protected the inhabitants.

Everything changed following the Six Day War. The Yattir forest was opened to visitors and the forester's house was turned into living quarters for youth groups and volunteers

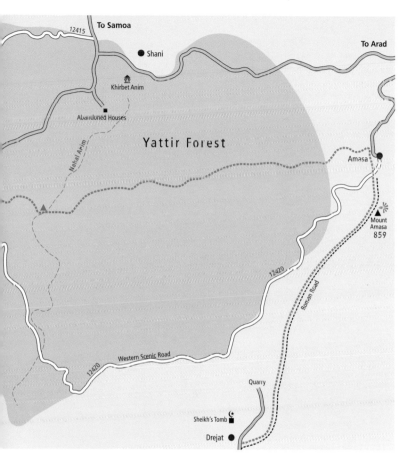

who came to work in the forest. The intifada changed all that and today the house again serves as a center for the foresters working in the area. In any case, the view from the roof of the building is magnificent.

In recent years, an additional use has been found for the forester's house: One of the rooms in it has been made available, at no charge, to hikers along the Israel Trail. The room has two beds, a bathroom with a toilet and shower, and a coffee corner.

From the forester's house, the Israel Trail

crosses the paved road that cuts through the forest and descends along a dirt path. To the right, as usual, are pine trees that were planted here. To the left is an interesting grove of pistachios and Atlantic pistachios (*ela Atlantit* in Hebrew). It is easy to tell the difference between them – the pistachio's leaves are much broader.

From here onward, in the valleys we can see the vineyards of the communities of the southern Hebron Hills. The Yattir winery uses their grapes to make wine.

One of the valleys was formed in the shallow channel of Nahal Anim. The Israel Trail passes through the riverbed alongside the remains of a stone road that, of course, also comes with an interesting story. In winter, it was difficult for the workers in the forest to drive their trucks through the muddy riverbed and so they paved the path with stones.

By the channel to Nahal Anim, the Israel Trail passes a path labeled with a red X. In order to keep hikers from getting confused and wandering off the marked trail, red Xs are being placed at strategic points along the Israel Trail.

The path continues, between forests of pine and cypress trees, to the scenic eastern road (with red markings). To the left is the small community of Amasa. The residents generously decided to make an empty room in the middle of the community available to hikers at no charge. The room has two beds, a kitchenette, a bathroom with a shower, and a few books. Hikers who arrive at night can call the community's night watchman, whose phone number is posted on the gate.

The Israel Trail continues to gently climb Mount Amasa on an amazingly well-preserved Roman road that is five meters wide.

Mount Amasa is a nature reserve in which Mediterranean and desert plants meet, making it a great place to see flowers in spring. The flowers here include the phlomis pungens (*shalhavit hagalgal* in Hebrew) and the wild almond (*shaked katan alim* in Hebrew).

Near the summit of Mount Amasa, the Israel Trail leaves the Roman road and leads us to the highest point on the ridge, which offers a view of the Judean Desert, the modern town of Arad, and Tel Arad.

The trail then returns to the Roman road, which passes the watershed line of a stream that descends to a large quarry that is operating at full force. At the quarry, the trail leaves the Roman road, bypasses the quarry, and continues through a corridor to its east. End your hike at the approach road to the quarry, not far from the village of Drejat, whose name is inspired by the Roman road.

A pistachio grove.

Hurvat Yattir.

Sunset in Drejat.

Route 21:
Across the Judean Desert on Foot

Fascinating landscapes abound on the Judean Desert plateau. This route is for proficient hikers only.

Route length: 23 km.
Difficulty: For proficient hikers only.
Start point: The corner of Ahva and Tzabar streets, Arad. Take the main entrance into Arad, turn right (opposite the Inbar Hotel) on Yehuda Street and drive along it to Ahva Street. The street is built in the upper segment of the channel of Nahal Tabiya. Descend to Tzabar Street and begin to walk beside the little corner with the benches.
Access: From Arad.
End point: Western Masada campsite.
Duration: 10-11 hours.
Admission fees: None.
Opening hours: None.
Equipment: Comfortable walking shoes, a hat, a sufficient quantity of water, sunscreen, and food.
Remarks: Shmulik Shapira, director of safety for the Israel Nature and Parks Authority, hopes that after the necessary funds are obtained, safety improvement works will be carried out in the dangerous segments of the Elazar Ascent and it will again be possible to go down it.
Pickup point for cars: End of route.
Map: Southern Judean Desert and Dead Sea Hiking and Trail Map (No. 11).

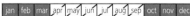

jan feb mar apr may jun jul aug sep oct nov dec

For the hikers among us, the phrase "Judean Desert" evokes images of deep canyons, steep ascents, and springs beside the Dead Sea. Some people speed along its thoroughfares in jeeps, but only a few cross the desert on foot from west to east. In just one day, a good hiker setting out from Arad can cross the desert, even diagonally, and reach Masada. The optimal time to do this is between October and March.

Begin at the riverbed of Nahal Tabiya, which descends southward from the center of Arad. After passing several benches and planted ornamental trees, you will suddenly lose sight of any sign of civilization and find yourselves walking down the riverbed. Like seven other routes around Arad, Nahal Tabiya was recently given trail markings (in its case, blue).

A green stripe of broad clotbur (*Xanthium strumarium*, or *lachid hanehalim* in Hebrew), a plant that grows in habitats in which there are seasonal water pools, attests to leaks in Arad's sewage disposal system.

Nahal Tabiya continues to wind its way several times between the hard, cracked limestone couches of the Kidud Ridge. Large bushes of white broom grow in the rock crevices, and in early winter, Day's marjoram (*Origanum dayi*, or *azuvit hamidbar* in Hebrew) blooms here, with aromatic leaves that make a nice addition to a cup of tea.

In the spot where Nahal Tabiya meets a little riverbed that comes from the left, just before it reaches Nahal Ye'elim (Riverbed of the Ibexes), grows a wonderful umbrella acacia (*Acacia tortilis*, or *shita sochachanit*). This is an ideal place to have breakfast.

In Nahal Ye'elim, the layers of hard limestone of the Kidud anticline vanish. This means that we had moved on to the area of the large syncline of the Judean Desert, which was covered mainly in the Cenozoic era (88-65 million years ago) with sediments of bright, soft chalk. The Byzantine-period inhabitants of this area realized that soft chalk is impermeable to water and made good use of this knowledge.

After walking about 200 meters, you will see on your left, behind a low wall made of rocks at the bottom of a light-colored rock cliff, an opening leading to a large cistern: the Kidud *ma'agora*. A *ma'agora* is a special kind of cistern hewn in the side of a riverbed, slightly above the level of the riverbed. It is a large chamber, whose ceiling is the natural rock; if necessary, the hewers of the cistern left rock columns in it to support the ceiling. The *ma'agora* collects floodwater from a higher point in the riverbed by means of a diversion canal. The Kidud *ma'agora* is very large – about 14 meters long. A great deal of silt covers its floor, but judging from other *ma'agorot*, it is about 5 meters deep.

Continue walking down Nahal Ye'elim for about another 200 meters to reach a trail marked in red on the right. Turn onto the red trail, which continues along Nahal Ye'elim. After about one kilometer, you will reach a Bedouin settlement built of tin huts. The Bedouins are very suspicious of strangers as there is an ongoing struggle over land in this area between the members of the tribe and the Israeli authorities.

Continue along the riverbed of Nahal Ye'elim. This riverbed passes along the seam between the Hatrurim rock formation and the chalk plateau north of it. Hatrurim is a unique formation of a variety of rocks in an assortment of color configurations.

When Nahal Ye'elim makes a wide turn to the right, the trail cuts across the bend and climbs up a low ridge to shorten the way. From here, it crosses Nahal Ye'elim from south to north in order to ascend a *nakab* in the wall of hills that encloses the area from the north. *Nakab* is an Arabic term for a natural passage in a mountainous area that is wide enough for a camel to pass through. The word is very similar to the ancient Hebrew word *nakubta*.

From this point, you are surrounded by a clean and beautiful desert. Follow the *nakab* along the periphery of the Kena'im anticline, made of hard limestone and dolomite. In the highest part, on the right side, clusters of flint stones mark an ancient Bedouin cemetery. After 100 meters, you will come across huge bulblike masses of rock more than a meter in diameter.

This is the point to stop and look at the landscape before descending. To the east is the Dead Sea, with the wall of the Mountains of Moab behind it. To the north is the continuation of the Kena'im anticline. The narrow canyons of Nahal Kidud and Nahal Menahem burst out of the anticline and unite at its foot into a broad valley, which links up with Nahal Rahaf. The edge of Nahal Rahaf's canyon, which cuts through He'etekim Cliff above the Dead Sea, can also be seen. At the foot of the *nakab* grows a jujube tree, providing shade that is a dream come true for every desert hiker.

Leave the shade of the tree and set off to cross the valley at the foot of the Kena'im anticline. Circumvent Mt. Yonatan from the south. Mt. Yonatan is typical of the Judean

Desert's residual hills: the rock around it eroded and it was left standing alone.

Descend to Nahal Emunim, where an umbrella acacia grows about 70 meters to the right of the trail. The trail crosses a dirt road for 4x4 vehicles, marked in green,

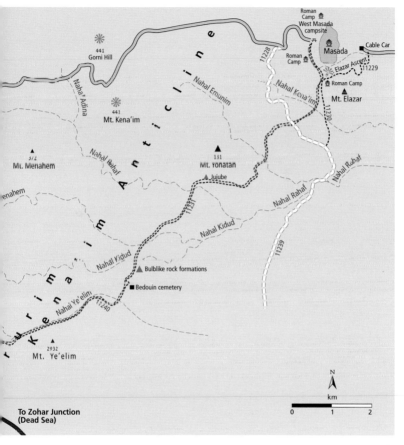

which links the western part of Masada with the Arad-Dead Sea Highway. Climb the saddle at the foot of Mt. Elazar. A bit before the ascent, the red trail joins up with a trail marked in black. The end of the ascent is a lookout point that offers a spectacular view of Masada.

Continue on the red trail, along the Roman ramp, passing the steep cliff that creates the gorge separating Mt. Elazar from Masada, and end the hike on Masada's western side.

Route 22:

The Gorges of Nahal Mishmar

A hike along the riverbeds of Nahal Tze'elim and Nahal Mishmar in the Dead Sea region, including an exciting new trail through a beautiful and challenging gorge.

Route length: 15 km.

Difficulty: For proficient hikers. Includes climbing up the northern Tze'elim Ascent, descending a very steep slope on the southern Mishmar Ascent to Ein Mishmar, and then negotiating a crevice of Nahal Mishmar with the aid of spikes.

Start point: Sayeret Nahal Tze'elim campsite.

Access: Route 90, south of kilometer marker 231.

End point: Nahal Mishmar campsite.

Duration: 8 hours.

Admission fees: None.

Opening hours: None.

Equipment: Good walking shoes and sufficient water (at least 3 liters per person in winter).

Remarks: Option of a short hike (4 hours): Climb from the Nahal Mishmar campsite on the riverbed's northern bank (trail marked in red) to the top of the gorge and descend into the gorge on the trail marked in blue.

Pickup point for cars: End of route.

Map: Southern Judean Desert and Dead Sea Hiking and Trail Map (11).

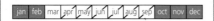

jan | feb | mar | apr | may | jun | jul | aug | sep | oct | nov | dec

Begin this hike by spending a quiet night in the campsite in Nahal Tze'elim (Riverbed of Acacias). A stroll before sunset on the riverbed's huge alluvial fan, the delta-like plain through which its flash floods empty into the Dead Sea, northeast of Masada, is a nice way to get into the mood for the next day's hike. The alluvial fan is created by silt deposited on the flat, open plain after the river emerges from the mountains.

An alluvial fan of a Judean Desert riverbed is a fascinating phenomenon, a world alternately built and destroyed with great frequency. For example, the huge acacia tree that grows at the eastern edge of the alluvial fan in Nahal Tze'elim is green and healthy-looking, thanks to a little channel that brings it sizable amounts of water. But in another year or two, perhaps 20, everything can change. The channel might be blocked up with silt, cutting off the tree from its water source. On the other hand, a torrential flood could come along and uproot the tree. The acacias and other desert shrubbery that develops in an alluvial fan serve as an important source of food for insects, birds, and other creatures.

Nahal Tze'elim canyon.

The Nahal Tze'elim alluvial fan is a habitat for rodents, hares, and gazelles, and hyena tracks are not hard to find.

In the past, the alluvial fans of the Judean Desert riverbeds reached the Dead Sea shore. Recently, the shore has become elusive, due to the sharp drop in the level of the lake. The Dead Sea is in a sad state of affairs for a lake situated in one of the world's most dramatic settings.

Nahal Tze'elim

Nahal Tze'elim is 32 kilometers long, beginning near Arad and ending at the Dead Sea. A dirt road (Route 11101) marked in black leads from Route 90, along the Dead Sea (just south of kilometer marker 231), to the Nahal Tze'elim campsite. The edge of the campsite, defined by a line of large rocks, overlooks the riverbed, bursting out of the He'etekim Cliff.

From the campsite, a trail marked in green climbs northward up the slope of the riverbed, and after about half a kilometer meets up with a trail marked in blue. The blue trail, the northern Tze'elim Ascent (trail 11131), spans a height differential of 400 meters. It is one of the oldest "modern" ascents of the Judean Desert, created as a mule run in the 1950s to haul provisions to the archaeological expedition that explored the nearby caves. Nahal Tze'elim contains a relatively large number of water sources – the springs of Ein Aneva and Ein Nammer (Leopard Spring), and the Nammer Pool. The trails leading to the springs were used by shepherds and their flocks.

The ascent, along a little ravine, is quite steep. Several acacias have clung to the banks of the ravine, but since water is scarce here, they are the size of bushes. Before the trail ends, it passes through a rock crevice and rises to the top of the Judean Desert Plateau.

At the top of the plateau, veer a bit to the left, to the edge of the cliff, and gaze down into the Tze'elim canyon. From here, you can see the mouth of Nahal Tze'elim, the northern wing of Masada, and the trail leading from Ein Aneva to the fortress. The Roman soldiers probably made their way along this trail when they brought water from the springs to the fighters besieging the Jews bastioned on the mountain.

The trail continues northward, parallel to the He'etekim Cliff. After passing the green-marked trail leading to Ein Nammer, you arrive at a dirt road marked in blue. It leads up a hill to a spot with a fabulous view of the expanses of the Judean Desert, including Mt. Hidai, Mt. Rivai, and Mt. Itai, which serve as important orientation points. The hotels of Arad, as well as Masada and the Roman ramp, can also be seen from this lookout point.

Now continue on the black trail (trail 11127). The trail reaches a dirt road, which leads to the edge of the cliff. The road has a "transparent" marking (two white stripes with no colored stripe in the center), inviting hikers to make a small detour from the main trail in order to reach a spring, an archaeological site, a lookout point, or another point of interest. The markings along the dirt path lead to a lookout point with an amazing view of the canyon of Nahal Mishmar and Me'arat Hamatmon (Cave of the Treasure).

The cave lies 50 meters from the top of the cliff and about 250 meters above the

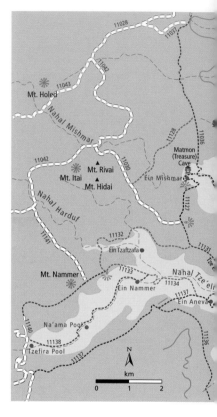

floor of Nahal Mishmar, from where the little spring of Ein Mishmar emanates. It's hard to believe that humans ever lived here, especially since no trail to the cave can be seen. Experts conjecture that even in ancient times only a narrow ledge offered access to the cave; the ledge was apparently destroyed.

gist Prof. Yochanan Aharoni, conducted a 10-day survey in the caves in Nahal Tze'elim and discovered many finds.

The discovery, writes Yosef Aviram in *Me'arot Midbar Yehuda* (Caves of the Judean Desert), aroused a great deal of interest. Prime Minister David Ben-Gurion ordered the Israel Defense Forces to make available the necessary means for carrying out a comprehensive survey in all of the riverbeds between Ein Gedi and Masada. So began "Operation Judean Desert." It was perhaps the most complex archaeological expedition that had ever been carried out in Israel.

Some 60 kibbutzniks, 20 students, and 80 soldiers took part in the first stage. They worked in very harsh conditions for two weeks and slept in camps set up by the army on the desert plateau. The operation was kept secret for security reasons (the survey was conducted close to what was then the border with Jordan) and to avoid arousing curiosity.

After many days of disappointment, the members of the team were rewarded when they discovered, in the caves of Nahal Hever, letters that proved once and for all that Bar Kochba was indeed a historical figure and not just a legend.

Despite the many finds, it was clear that another operation was needed. For the second stage of Operation Judean Desert, 300 people were enlisted. Archaeologist Pesach Bar-Adon was in charge of the survey of the Nahal Mishmar region, and the expedition's encampment was above a cave in the riverbed known as Me'arat Hasayarim (Cave of the Scouts).

By the seventh day of the dig, the exca-

Quest for Scrolls

In the 1950s, antiquities from the period of the Bar Kochba rebellion began to appear on the market. Archaeologists suspected that the source of these items were the caves of Nahal Tze'elim and other Judean Desert caves. In January 1960, an expedition with 25 participants, led by archaeolo-

A squill in bloom.

Dead Acacia.

vators decided that there was no point in continuing, since the finds were modest and insignificant. But just when they were dismantling the encampment, a call came from the telephone that the army had installed in the cave. Bar-Adon reported the discovery of a cache of dozens of copper objects and asked that a photographer be sent the next morning in order to document the finds.

That night, the dig participants were too excited to sleep. The first thing in the morning, the excavators resumed their work. Three and a half hours later, they extracted no less than 439 objects from a bundle wrapped in a small mat. The objects, made mostly of copper, were beautiful and well-preserved and included statues of birds and other animals. In the evening, the items were displayed in the encampment, and the cave's name was changed to Me'arat Hamatmon (Cave of the Treasure).

The cache is attributed to the Chalcolithic period (about 5,000 years ago). The objects are of uncertain origins, but they attest to a material culture of a high level. It is assumed that they were ritual articles, which may have been used by the priests of the Chalcolithic temple in Ein Gedi; it may have been the priests who buried them in the cave. One thing is clear: after

Nahal Mishmar.

The Cave of the Treasure.

the objects were buried, no human being ever set foot in the cave again.

Nahal Mishmar

From the lookout point, return to the black trail and followed it down into the canyon of Nahal Mishmar. The steep trail, sometimes very narrow, leads directly to the tiny perennial spring of Ein Mishmar. Martins come there to drink and hunt insects, and dragonflies hover over the water. In the rock to the right, from which a thin jet of water falls, a huge lilac chaste tree grows. A family of Syrian hyraxes dwells near the spring and it can be assumed that other animals also come here to quench their thirst. However, the main attraction of the spring is its lovely setting, at the foot of an enormous dry waterfall. The black trail meets up with a red trail (trail 11126) that circumvents the gorge of Nahal Mishmar and leads down to the riverbed's campsite. The more adventurous should choose a new trail, marked in blue (11125), that leads through the Mishmar gorge. It's a memorable walk. The gorge narrows to a meter or two, a crevice with a wall so steep that a ladder with 22 metal spikes has been installed for hikers – a grand finale for the hike. Once out of the canyon a final 2 kilometers walk will bring you to the Nahal Mishmar Campsite, the end of our hike.

Route 23:
The Pools of Nahal Ashalim

Nahal Ashalim is one of Israel's most famous desert riverbeds, thanks mainly to its many pools, which fill up with water each winter. At that time of year, this challenging route for experienced hikers involves not only hiking, but also swimming.

Route length: 10 km from the Nahal Azgad parking area (accessible to 4x4s and very sturdy cars) and 14 km (2 km extra in each direction) from the pumping station (accessible to buses).

Difficulty: For proficient hikers and swimmers.

Start point: Nahal Azgad parking area.

Access: Route 90, opposite Dead Sea Works.

End point: Nahal Azgad parking area.

Duration: Seven hours when there isn't water in the pools and nine hours when there is. Large groups should add two hours.

Admission fees: None.

Opening hours: None.

Equipment: Shoes for walking in water and a waterproof bag for food and equipment that could be damaged by water. A 20-meter rope is also recommended.

Remarks: Do not set out on this tour when there is a danger of rain and flash floods.

Pickup point for cars: End of route.

Map: Southern Judean Desert and Dead Sea Hiking and Trail Map (11).

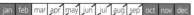

jan | feb | mar | apr | may | jun | jul | aug | sep | oct | nov | dec

The trip to the starting point where a hike begins is usually the worst part of an excursion for hikers. However, in this case, it actually is quite enjoyable, at least the part during which you travel west on the road with red trail markings (opposite the Dead Sea Works on Route 90, between kilometer markers 193 and 194, unpaved road 11419). The road leads to the Amiaz Plain. This is where the famous flour cave, which attracted many hikers before it was closed to visitors because some sections in it collapsed, is located. The Amiaz Plain is made of soft, white marl. During the War of Independence, it was used as a landing strip for light aircrafts, which brought supplies and weapons to besieged Sdom. The name Amiaz is reminiscent of the Arab name for the area: Satah al-Amiaz.

After traveling about five kilometers on the red marked road, you reach an intersection with a large campground next to it. Continue west on the path with black trail markers. After about 500 meters, another campground is reached that is more intimate and suitable for a small group of hikers. Further on is the Periclas pumping station, which conveys the minerals pumped from the Dead Sea to the factories on the Rotem Plain. The pipe, which runs westward from here and ascends the escarpment of the Hatzera Ridge, is pretty well camouflaged, but still discernible.

At the next intersection, we arrive at the black-marked path that ascends Ma'aleh Azgad and climbs to the area where the Rotem Plain factories are located. However, instead of following it, descend along the red-marked trail to the riverbed of Nahal Azgad and park next to the Amiaz Five pumping station. In ancient times, this road was part of the route that led from the shores of the Dead Sea to Tel Malhata in the Beersheba Valley.

Nahal Azgad

A path with green trail markings leads into the channel of Nahal Azgad, which for some reason is named after a biblical family from Judah which was among those who returned to Zion from the Babylonian exile (Ezra 2:12).

After we pass through the waves of dust caused by the drilling at Amiaz Five, an enchanting narrow riverbed that has acacia raddiana (*shita slilnit* in Hebrew) and a single jujube (*shizif* in Hebrew) growing in it is reached.

The riverbed is full of small rockfalls. The beginning of the path bypasses them from the left. Later, when there is a longer series of rockfalls in the riverbed, the path leaves the riverbed completely, continuing for a while on the southern slope. This part of the path is steep and you will have to use your hands to climb it.

The path then returns to the riverbed, crosses it, bypasses a large rockfall on the northern bank, and returns to the riverbed. The channel then becomes shallow, a hint that we are near the head of the river. One more rockfall awaits us, which is very high. There is no choice at this point but to leave the riverbed. The path bypasses the rockfall from the south, and then climbs the slope to the left of the red-marked path. We now find ourselves on a narrow rise that separates Nahal Azgad from the huge channel of Nahal Ashalim.

Nahal Ashalim.

Nahal Ashalim

The red-marked path (11442) goes west, crossing the rise and providing a view of both the riverbeds. We are directly above the huge rockfall in Nahal Ashalim. This riverbed begins by the Periclas factory, cuts across the extensions of the Hatzera Ridge, and finally arrives at this point. Its Hebrew name is a translation of the Arabic name, Wadi Umm Tafpa, which means Mother of the Tamarisks Riverbed.

The red path descends to the riverbed. The

descent is very steep and a long ladder has been put here to help. Some hikers can't restrain themselves from approaching the top of the cliff face, which plunges down more than 100 meters. The view is probably amazing, but it is extremely dangerous to check it out. Some very brave hikers have tried crawling to the edge to peek over, but even that really isn't recommended.

In order to bypass the rockfall and reach the riverbed at the bottom of it, climb the steep blue-marked path (11445) on the

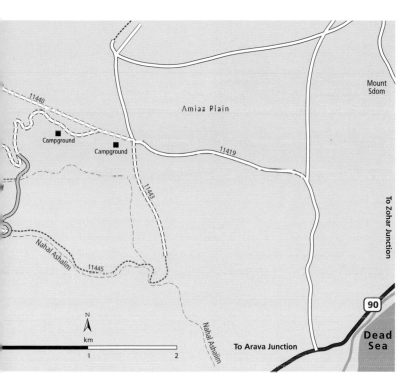

southern bank of Nahal Ashalim. From the top of the path, the pools of the Dead Sea Works and the tongue of the Dead Sea, the southern edge of Mount Sdom, the upper tributaries of Nahal Hamarmar, Jordan's a-Safi oasis and the beginning of Nahal Zered, the Moab Mountains, and — of course — the Nahal Ashalim landscape can be seen. Before continuing, turn left and walk for a minute or two to the edge of the ridge to an amazing viewpoint of the canyon and the big rockfall.

The descent to the channel of the riverbed is very steep. Just at the beginning of the path is a Syrian sumac (*og kotzani* in Hebrew and *rhus tripartita* in Latin), a tree which rarely grows in this area. It generally is found in the deserts of Samaria and Judea, Har Hanegev, and western Samaria.

There also is a great view of the rockfall from here. The big green blur at its foot is a clump of toothbrush trees (*salvadora Parsit* in Hebrew and *salvadora persica* in Latin).

An expanse of rock greets us in the

View of Nahal Ashalim area.

riverbed. The canyon floor is located between walls that are more than 100 meters high. At the beginning, the path is to the left of the riverbed, allowing access along the riverbed, instead of through the many pools and craters.

The famous gorge of Nahal Ashalim – a narrow canyon that is about 1.5 km long and 40 meters deep – is quickly reached. After the winter rains, the pools fill with water, which remains in the riverbed for several months. Several pools are quite large and hikers need to swim to cross them, which turns this hike into a challenging experience.

The canyon is divided into two parts. The upper part is longer. Then the riverbed is in the open for a short distance before entering another canyon. An especially large toothbrush tree grows in this canyon. Those who are brave enough to climb to the point it grows from will find that it has an especially thick, impressive stem with a 1.5 meter circumference.

The rockfalls along this section of the hike aren't especially high. Athletic hikers can handle them without any special equipment, though using a rope will make things easier. The last significant pool is large, round, and completely surrounded by slippery walls. The rope that is usually stretched across this pool makes crossing it easier.

Now all that remains is the walk back to the car. We walk by the pumping station, which lost a few of the mines that were part of its security system in one of the winter storms – this explains why entry to the riverbed beyond the point indicated by the path with red trail markings is forbidden. We walk northward on the path for about a kilometer until reaching Nahal Azgad, where we left the car.

Route 24:
The Pools of Nahal Peres

Families that enjoy hiking together will find this desert excursion to Nahal Peres rewarding. The route is easy, the views are spectacular, and in winter daring kids can even take a dip in the pools.

Route length: 10 km.
Difficulty: Families. Recommended for children over nine years of age.
Start point: The parking area that is beside kilometer marker 111 on the Dimona-Dead Sea Road (Route 25).
Access: Route 25.
End point: The Arava Junction.
Duration: 4 hours.
Admission fees: None.
Opening hours: None.
Equipment: Comfortable walking shoes, a hat, bathing suit, water, and food. If you like, bring along a gas ring in order to make coffee and tea.
Remarks: None.
Pickup point for cars: End of route.
Map: Southern Judean Desert and Dead Sea Hiking and Trail Map (11).

jan | feb | mar | apr | may | jun | jul | aug | sep | oct | nov | dec

Nahal Peres drains from the eastern slopes of the Hatzera ridge and extends for some 17 kilometers. There are hiking trails along most of it, but when hikers talk about Nahal Peres, they usually mean the lower part of the riverbed. This is a pleasant, easy route that passes waterholes and runs through a narrow gorge. The landscape is impressive and fun to walk through and the hike draws to its close at a lookout point with a spectacular view of the southern Dead Sea and the mountains of Edom and Moab.

The Hike

The trail, with red markings (11537), begins in the parking area and leads to one of the tributaries of Nahal Peres. This point offers a view of the clean white desert, with acacia trees growing in the riverbed. On the other side of the riverbed Mt. Zurim rises to a height of 78 meters above sea level. The mountain's table-like shape is typical of many mountains in the Negev due to the layer of hard rock that covers the soft chalk of the mountain, preventing erosion.

The black-marked trail that begins here descends into the riverbed's eastern tributary, bypassing the pools. Continue along the red trail, which leads past the black trail and a dirt road marked in blue. The trail climbs a bit and then arrives at Nahal Peres, reaching the top of the gorge in

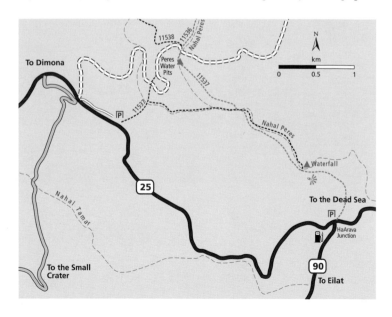

which the pools are located.

The winter rains make this point the highlight of the hike. In the center of a 100-meter-long rocky area is a string of pools that fill with water in the winter. It is framed on both sides by 8-meter high banks. A 10-meter-high waterfall adds a final touch to the charm of this site.

This is a great place for a long break, including a dip in the pools and a picnic. The high banks provide shade and the area radiates tranquility.

After enjoying the pools, continue along the green-marked trail, bypassing the waterfall from the left, to the point where it meets the black-marked trail.

Follow the black-marked trail into the riverbed. The trail now leads through a narrow gorge for about half a kilometer, passing many small pools.

Some 80 meters before a large waterfall, 50 meters above the riverbed, the black-marked path leaves the channel, veering to the right, up a ladder of metal rungs attached to the rock. Climb the ladder to the green-marked trail leading to the top of the Peres Ascent.

You are now standing on the remains of an ancient road that led from the Tamar Fortress to the oasis of Zo'ar. The view of the Dead Sea and the mountains of Moab and Edom is spectacular. From here, the trail descends to the parking area beside the Arava Junction, where the hike ends.

Pools of Nahal Peres.

Rappeling at Nahal Peres.

Route 25:
The Colors of the Negev

A 20-kilometer hike across the Small Makhtesh for good walkers.

Route length: 20 km.
Difficulty: For good hikers.
Start point: Eli Ascent.
Access: From the Ma'aleh Akrabim Road (Route 227).
End point: The exit of Nahal Mazar.
Duration: 9-10 hours. Shorter six-hour option: Walk from the Tamar Fortress to Ein Tzafit in Nahal Tzafit, go to the top of the Hatzera Ascent, and continue on the green trail to Nahal Mazar. Arrange to be picked up at the end of Nahal Mazar.
Admission fees: None.
Opening hours: None.
Equipment: Shoes for walking in water and a waterproof bag for food and equipment that could be damaged by water. A 20-meter rope is also recommended.
Remarks: Arrange to have a car waiting for you at the end of the route. Access and pickup roads are suitable for all vehicles.
Pickup point for cars: The exit of Nahal Mazar. Access is from the road to the Small Makhtesh branching off from the Dimona-Sdom Road (Route 25).
Map: Northern Arava and Eastern Negev Hiking and Trail Map (14).

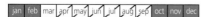

jan | feb | mar | apr | may | jun | jul | aug | sep | oct | nov | dec

To get to the starting point of this hike take Route 25 past Dimona to the Rotem Junction. Turn right at the junction and drive down Route 206 in the direction of Oron. Follow the road for 9 km and take the unpaved road to your left towards the Ma'leh Akrabim Junction. This road (Route 227) is the old British Mandate road to Eilat, descending to the Arava via Scorpions' Ascent. The road runs through the Yamin Plain, a 70-square-kilometer sandy plain that covers the valley between the Halira and Halzera ranges. After crossing the plain, the road begins to climb the Hatzera range along the riverbed of Nahal Ma'aleh.

At the crest of the range, the road reaches an unpaved road, marked in red that leads off to the left (trail 14155). Follow the red road for about a kilometer, to the spot where the hike begins. (Do not leave your car here. The driver should drive to the pick up point and wait there.)

Walk along the red road, up a gentle slope, amid shrubs of bean-capers, to the top of the Eli Ascent. The Small Makhtesh is spread out below in all of its splendor. The Small Makhtesh is one of those unique Negev depressions in which thousands of years of geological history are exposed. A makhtesh is drained by a single riverbed, in this case Nahal Hatzera.

The Eli Ascent is not an ancient passageway through the mountains: it was cleared by modern hikers in the 1950s. They named it Eli (Hebrew for pestle) because it leads down to a makhtesh (which literally means mortar, due to its bowl-like shape). Designed for hikers rather than for the heavily laden camels that plied such ascents in days gone by, it covers the 400-meter height differential via a very steep route, eased by stakes and railings.

After negotiating the limestone rock from the Cenomanian epoch (100 million years ago) at the beginning of the descent, you slide down a segment of sticky, muddy green clay and reach the colorful layers of sandstone that occupy about two-thirds of the cross section of the makhtesh cliff.

On the makhtesh floor, the trail leading to the opening of the makhtesh is marked on a silt step a bit higher than the riverbed around it. Most hikers, however, prefer to walk in one of the small riverbeds parallel to the trail, where a greater amount of colored rock is exposed. The many marks etched into the thin crust on the brittle sandstone attest to this practice.

The sandstone is coated with a thin patina that is usually light brown, a hue that is different from the color of the rock itself. Known as desert patina, desert lacquer, or desert rust, this coating is characteristic of exposed rock in the desert.

The color usually comes from ferric and manganese oxides, as well as other elements, such as copper and cobalt. It is generally thought that dew and rain seep into the rock and dissolve a few of its components. When the sun heats up the rock, the solutions rise to the surface. The water evaporates and leaves sediments that produce the desert patina.

Biological processes also play a part: beneath the desert patina are lichens, fungi, and algae that are capable of oxidizing elements such as oxygen and iron.

Over the ages, the patinas that coat the rocks became the billboards of the desert. Local inhabitants expressed their feelings in pictures carved into the patina, and simple inscriptions incised by pilgrims became historical testimony. But these ancient etchings do not justify such acts by modern schoolchildren, who deface the riverbeds with their graffiti.

The riverbeds are truly lovely. Their walls expose rock in spectacular colors: red, yellow, white, brown, and everything in between. The colors of the sandstone were produced by iron oxides, born of the erosion of minerals brought here via riverbeds from the Arabo-Nubian Massif.

The red trail meets up with Nahal Hatzera a bit before the opening of the makhtesh. You can tell that you are nearing a large riverbed by the presence of tamarisk trees, which grow in alluvial soil. An earth embankment with a breach in it, erected in the riverbed to halt the floodwaters and force them to seep into the aquifer, is crossed before the riverbed of Nahal Hatzera.

Nahal Hatzera is broad enough to host several spiraled acacias, 4 meters in height. Arabian babblers dwell in the vicinity of the trees.

A bit before the opening of the makhtesh, the red trail meets up with a trail marked in blue. A sign directs visitors to the Hatzera Ascent, which leads up from the makhtesh on its northern wall. Also at this spot is a small, fenced-in structure housing a pump that draws water from a well, hence the dam we saw earlier. The water is piped to a pool on Mt. Tzafit and

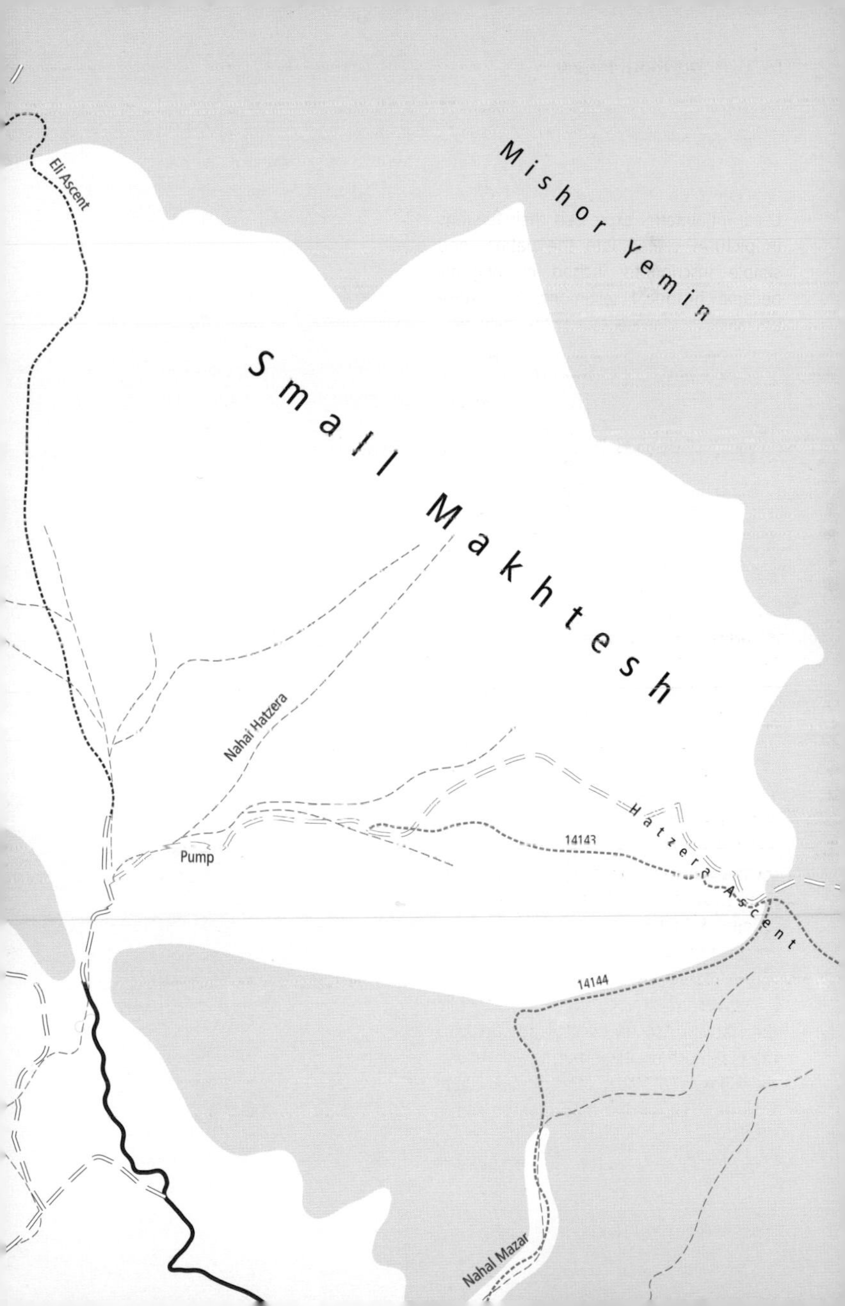

Eil Accent

Mishor Yemin

Small Makhtesh

Nahal Hatzera

Pump

Hatzera Ascent

14143

14144

Nahal Mazar

then to the factories on the Rotem Plain.

The blue trail leads up a shallow riverbed that drains the northern part of the makhtesh. After a short distance, the trail leaves the riverbed and leads up a dirt road. In the distance, the large spur of rock along which the Hatzera Ascent negotiates the makhtesh cliff can be easily discerned. A bit further away from it is an extremely steep dirt road, which accompanies the pipe extending from the well to the top of the makhtesh.

The blue trail (14143) now ascends the Hatzera Ascent. The cleared stones from the path and the gentleness of the curves indicate the ascent's antiquity. This is a real camel pass, part of the road that led to the makhtesh and the Arava from the Tamar Fortress, situated to the north.

After a difficult climb, the trail turns westward, atop the vertical Cenomanian limestone cliff that surrounds the makhtesh. At the bend in the trail, the Hatzera Ascent unites with the steep dirt road that accompanies the water pipe. Soon we reach a blockade comprising pipes, which is meant to prevent uninvited jeeps from going any further. The steep road is too

Small Makhtesh.

dangerous for all terrain vehicles.

At the top of the ascent is a stone monument to a young man who died of dehydration at that spot – a chilling reminder to take plenty of water to drink on this route. It's in a desert, after all.

Now comes a change in direction, as we take the green trail (14144) which leads eastward. The trail leads straight up to the top of the slope. Here, on the crest of the mountain right on the edge of the makhtesh, is a fabulous lookout point.

On one side, the makhtesh in its entirety can be seen; on the other, the grooved

expanses of marl in the Dead Sea Valley, the oasis of a-Safi, and the Jordanian potash plant, as well as Nahal Zered, which separates the mountains of Edom from the mountains of Moab.

Now continue on the easy green trail along the top of the cliff that surrounds the makhtesh and view the magnificent scenery. It is one of the most beautiful trails in the Negev.

Follow the trail for 2 kilometers as it leaves the cliff edge and descends to the top of Nahal Mazar, which begins as a shallow, stony channel. About 100 meters before an impassable waterfall, the trail turns left in order to circumvent it. Before continuing with the trail, walk in the direction of the waterfall. On the right bank of the riverbed is a stone shelf that affords a lovely view of the waterfall and the enormous rock cubes that lie at its foot. It's a wonderful place for a little rest.

Now return to the trail, circumvent the waterfall, and return to the riverbed, which is so broad at this point that little acacias grow in it. The floor of the riverbed gradually takes on the sharp incline of the steep hogbacks of the eastern slope of the Hatzera Ridge. The closer you get to the exit of the riverbed, the more inclined the layers.

Suddenly, the riverbed makes a heroic dive into the "crust" of the Hatzera Ridge, which is very steep here, creating a series of waterfalls and pits. The trail makes a steep descent to the right and reaches the exit of the riverbed. Another 150 meters to the left will bring you to the road leading to the Small Makhtesh, the end point of the hike.

Route 26:
The Barak Canyon

The cliffs along the Arava are studded with potholed canyons that fill with water after the rains. The white chalk of the Barak Canyon is spectacular.

Route length: 8 km.
Difficulty: Rope climbing, swimming, and rock scrambling.
Start point: Entrance to Barak Canyon.
Access: Kilometer marker 115 on the Arava Road (Route 90).
End point: Ring route.
Duration: 4-6 hours.
Admission fees: None.
Opening hours: None.
Equipment: Bathing suit and wading shoes. A safety rope is recommended.
Remarks: The climb through the canyon entails climbing rope ladders, ropes, and ordinary ladders as well as swimming across deep potholes.
Pickup point for cars: End of route.
Map: Central Arava and Eastern Negev Highlands Hiking and Trail Map (No. 17).

jan | feb | mar | apr | may | jun | jul | aug | sep | oct | nov | dec

The potholes of the Barak Canyon don't fill with water every year. Even if it rains in the Arava, they will not necessarily fill with water. But if there is a cloudburst over the upper reaches of the river, even for just a few hours, usually water rushes down the canyon, depositing sand and mud in some of the potholes, cleaning out others, and leaving them full of water. The water will stay in the canyon for a few years, getting murkier and less appealing as the years between flash floods go by. The trick is to get to the canyon in the early summer after a flood; then the potholes are full of water and the trip through the canyon involves swimming and climbing up the dry waterfalls. One word of warning: the trip is not easy. An experienced rockclimber should accompany you and safety equipment is necessary. But this hike is one of the most enjoyable desert experiences in Israel.

To get to the canyon, take Route 90 south to Eilat. After the turn-off to Baldad, continue for another 8 km to kilometer marker 116. Some 900 meters further on, you will see a blue track (17430) running off to the right. Drive along the blue track as far as your driving skills will permit. Park and continue on foot. Unless you are an exceptional driver, or driving a jeep or a car that is not your own, you will have to walk for another 3 or 4 km to reach the canyon. It is a pleasant walk along the ever narrowing Barak Riverbed.

At the canyon, continue on the blue trail (17465), which is also followed by the Israel Trail through the canyon. This will take time and major climbing efforts. However, it is fun and can be done by active and agile people – including kids from the age of 12 and up.

Once at the top, leave the Israel Trail and the blue trail that continues to another canyon (the Vardit Canyon) and follow the green trail (17468) that leads back to the entrance to the canyon.

From here, tired and full of experiences, you will have to walk back to your car.

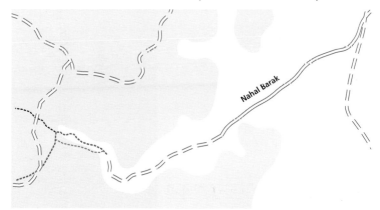

Nahal Barak

Route 27:
White Pools, Fake Marble, and Kings' Mothers

This pleasant 16-kilometer trek in the Negev takes hikers from the "Ashmadai Gate" to the "Marble Pools," the Zin Pools, and Ein Akrabim.

Route length: 16 km.
Difficulty: For good hikers. The path is pleasant, with few ascents and descents.
Start point: Entrance to the Small Makhtesh.
Access: The access road to the Small Makhtesh.
End point: The plateau above Ein Akrabim.
Duration: 6-8 hours.
Admission fees: None.
Opening hours: None.
Equipment: 5 liters of water per person, walking shoes, wading shoes, and mosquito repellent.
Remarks: Don't leave your car unguarded at the plateau above Ein Akrabim.
Pickup point for cars: From the bottom of Scorpions' Ascent (Route 227), take the black-marked unpaved road (14262) to its end.
Map: Northern Arava and Eastern Negev Hiking and Trail Map (14).

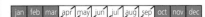

If you really want to understand the power of water, walk to the entrance of the Small Makhtesh and position yourself by the electricity pole situated there. Thirsty desert plants grow between the pole's metal rings to a height of 7 meters, which is the height of the water level during a flash flood. It is hard to believe that little Nahal Hatzera, which drains the water from the Small Makhtesh, could be that powerful.

Just by the entrance, a path with green trail markings (14260) descends into the riverbed of Nahal Hatzera. The riverbed forces its way through the same narrow pass that Palmach groups on training exercises traversed in the 1940s on their way to the depths of the Small Makhtesh. There were no roads in the area at that time, so the Palmach scouts made their way through the dry riverbed. They couldn't restrain themselves at the amazing sight of the makhtesh's walls and did what Palmachniks do best: they invented a myth. The evil Ashmadai, who wanted to destroy Solomon's Temple, dug a gigantic rock out of the earth in order to throw it at the Temple. The rock was so big that even he couldn't carry it for long and as he passed through here, his strength ran out and he was buried under the rock. The entrance to the riverbed is called Ashmadai's Gate in honor of the myth.

The green-marked path climbs to the plateau carved out by short streams, which descend from the slopes of the Small Makhtesh to Nahal Zin. Then the path joins the dirt path (with red trail markings) that runs along the high banks of the riverbed. After a while, it leaves the dirt path to descend to the broad stream of Nahal Zin.

The river ate into the bottom of its banks, which were made of a soft layer of clay. The layer of hard limestone above this layer creates a roof of sorts for about 70 meters. This is a great place to rest in the shade.

About 200 meters from here, we reached an amazing series of deep hollows, between prominent, polished white stones. To top it off, a stream flows through here. The clear water is actually effluent water that the phosphate factory at Nahal Zin emits after washing phosphate rock, a process that is intended to enrich the concentration of phosphorus in the rock. In other words, look but don't drink. This area is called the "Marble Pools," but the name is based on a small mistake. The rock is limestone, which looks similar to marble.

From here onward, we proceeded alongside the broad riverbed, where the seemingly innocuous stream of water carved 5-meter-high shoulders into the stone. To the right are the slopes of the Hatzera Ridge: layers of rock protruding skyward at sharp, strange angles. To the left, the ridge slowly fades away into the Arava and creates a region called the Yoadan Hills.

Consider the names in this area for a moment. Hatzera Ridge is a mispronunciation of the Arabic name Jebel Hadira, which means Pen Ridge. Indeed, the erect walls of the Small Makhtesh, which completely encircle the area beneath it, are reminiscent of an enclosure for livestock. It is a simple and clear explanation. The Yoadan Hills, however, are a whole different story.

Yoadan, or Jehoaddan, was the mother of King Amaziah of Judah. The main river into which the Yoadan Hills drain is Nahal Amaziah, flowing through the Arava past what was once the Dead Sea. Many of the small streams that flow into Nahal Amaziah from the Yoadan Hills are named for the mothers of the kings of Judah. Nahal Abi is named for the mother of King Hezekiah, Nahal Jecoliah for the mother of Uzziah, and Nahal Jerusha for the mother of Jotham. Amaziah became the name of the biggest river since he won a difficult battle against the Edomites for control of the Negev. "He slew of Edom in the Valley of Salt ten thousand, and took Sela by war, and called the name of it Joktheel, unto this day" (2 Kings 14:7).

In the Book of Chronicles (2:25), there is a detailed account of the battle, which ended with sending 10,000 of the people of Edom to their death from the top of a cliff. This place, Sela, marks the border between the Land of Canaan and the Land of Edom: "And the border of the Amorites was from the ascent of Akrabbim, from Sela, and upward" (Judg. 1:36).

Meanwhile, the path led us to another series of stone pits. These are smaller than the "marble" ones and have a logical name: the Zin Pools. Not far from here is a dam for measuring the level of the runoff water in Nahal Zin. The river is gorgeous at this point. A 10-meter-wide stream flows between low limestone shoulders, with the Hatzera Ridge in the background.

Not far past this segment, our path leaves the riverbed and enters the great salt marshes of Ein Zin and Ein Akrabim. Today, it is no longer possible to see real springs here. Like many of the "springs" in the Negev, Ein Akrabim is more a combination of wishful thinking and high groundwater than a true spring. And the freshwater of Ein Zin drowned long ago in the effluent water from the phosphate factory at Nahal Zin. However, the salt savannahs here are impressive, as are the plants such as the monoecious seabite and the coast aeluropus, and lots of tamarisk trees. The palm trees here stand out as in a child's drawing of the desert. One final warning: In recent years, this site has attracted hordes of monstrous mosquitoes that don't just sting – they declare war.

Nahal Zin.

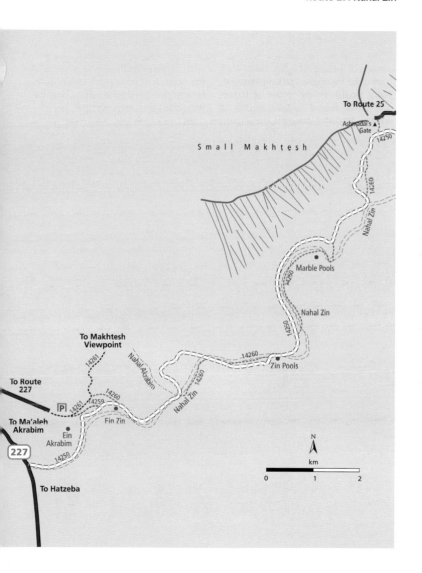

To Route 25

Ashmadai's
Gate

14250

Small Makhtesh

14260

Nahal Zin

Marble Pools

14260

Nahal Zin

14250

To Makhtesh
Viewpoint

14260

Zin Pools

14261

Nahal Akrabim

To Route
227

14260

14261

14259

Nahal Zin

P

To Ma'aleh
Akrabim

Fin Zin

Ein
Akrabim

227

N

14250

km

To Hatzeba

0   1   2

Route 28:
The Back Road to Avdat

A hike across Nahal Zin to the Ein Akev water hole and from there through desert ascents and back trails to the Nabatean city of Avdat.

Route length: 12 km.
Difficulty: Good hikers.
Start point: Zin Ascent.
Access: From Sdeh Boker.
End point: Avdat National Park.
Duration: 6 hours.
Admission fees: Admission charge to the national park.
Opening hours:
National parks are open:
April to Sept.: 8 a.m. - 5 p.m.,
Fri. and holiday eves until 4 p.m.
Oct. to Mar.: 8 a.m. - 4 p.m.,
Fri. and holiday eves until 3 p.m.
Equipment: Regular plus a bathing suit.
Remarks: Do not dive into the water at Ein Avdat. The pool is very deep with dangerous rocks inside it. Swimming is at your own risk.
Pickup point for cars: End of route.
Map: Central Negev Hiking and Trail Map (15).

jan | feb | mar | apr | may | jun | jul | aug | sep | oct | nov | dec

Start the hike at the bottom of the Zin Ascent. To get there, drive along the track marked in black (15375) that starts from Route 40 about 100 meters north of kilometer marker 131. The track, which can be traversed by ordinary vehicles driven by experienced drivers, runs along the northern fence of Midreshet Ben-Gurion and then along the cliff of Nahal Zin to a small airstrip. The track continues from the southern edge of the airstrip down into the Zin Valley. If you are an experienced driver, you can drive all the way to the bottom of the ascent, which is where our hike starts.

The Akev Needlepoint

Follow the green track (15372) that runs along the bottom of the cliffs to Ein Shaviv. The track runs along the old Eilat-Ashkelon pipeline that, many years ago in a different era, used to pipe the oil of Iran to the Mediterranean. One kilometer down the track, a red trail (15367) leads off to the right, climbing up to Hod Akev – the Akev Needlepoint

The summit of Hod Akev, 567 meters above sea level, offers a 360-degree view of the surroundings: Ramat Avdat with its table mountains to our south and the long anticlines of the northern Negev highlands to our north.

The red trail descends the other side of Hod Akev into Nahal Akev. The trail circumvents the protruding hill 514 from the north and meets up with the blue trail (15366) that runs from the Ein Akev parking lot (for jeeps) to the spring. Follow the blue trail upriver (left) to the

spring.

Ein Akev is a small spring that emanates from the side of the Zinim Cliff. Around the spring are water-loving desert plants. A small waterfall drips into the main pool at the bottom of the cliff. The spring is a source of sustenance for many different types of desert animals such as leopards, hyenas, foxes, and ibexes.

Upper Ein Akev

The blue trail climbs up to the flat area above the spring and reaches a trail junction. Continue south along the black trail (15362), which, after 3 kilometers, reaches a large group of reeds.

A small pool in between the reeds collects the waters of another spring — Upper Ein Akev. In the summer, many Bedouin shepherds come to the small pool to water their flocks.

Now take the blue trail (15363) to the right, up the western slope of Nahal Akev. Two kilometers later, once we are out of Nahal Akev, we will come upon an impressive series of agricultural terraces. These were the farming hinterland of Avdat during the Roman and Byzantine eras. Three kilometers later, the trail reaches the city of Avdat, inside the Avdat National Park. The trail passes an impressive Roman army camp (seldom seen by the regular visitors) and reaches the acropolis of the city with its churches, bathhouses, and ruins from the Roman and Byzantine eras. The park trails will lead you down the hill towards the entrance and the ticket booth.

If you are not interested in paying the park fee, take the black trail (15377) that circumvents the park and reaches the gas station on Route 40, near the entrance to the park.

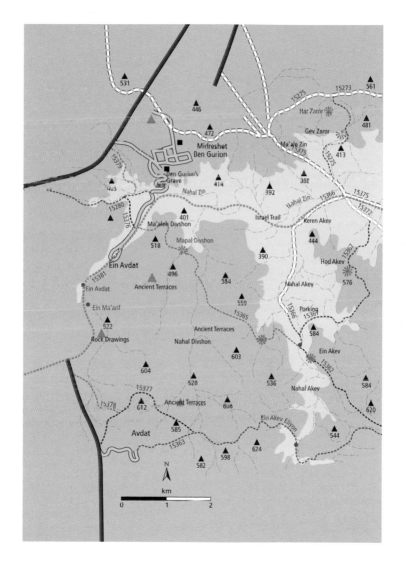

Route 29:
Up and Down the Coxcomb

The ERETZ staff set out for the Central Negev for a challenging hike on the Hatira Ridge, in the riverbeds of Nahal Mador and Nahal Afran.

Route length: 17 km.
Difficulty: The hike is for proficient hikers, not only because it is strenuous, but also because it requires skill to negotiate the steep slopes in Nahal Afran.
Start point: Blue trail up Nahal Mador.
Access: From the Oron phosphate plant, take the black unpaved road to Nahal Mador. A new jeep track circumvents the plant, which does not always allow hikers through the gate.
End point: Ring route.
Duration: 10 hours.
Admission fees: None.
Opening hours: None.
Equipment: Make sure to bring a flashlight in case you finish the hike in the dark.
Remarks: Please do not drive beyond the high-tension wire so as not to damage the natural landscape.
Pickup point for cars: Your pickup vehicle can shorten the way by 4 km if it waits for you near Nahal Afran. The beginning of the route can be reached in a sturdy vehicle or a 4x4.
Map: Central Negev Hiking and Trail Map (15).

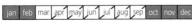

jan feb mar apr may jun jul aug sep oct nov dec

To get to the beginning of the route, take Route 206 from the Rotem Junction east of Dimona to Oron. Turn right (west) about 500 meters before the gate of the Oron plant onto a dirt road (marked in red) that bypasses the plant. Drive to the foot of the hill with the antenna on it and complete the bypass of the phosphate works from the north. Then the road crosses the railroad tracks and continues parallel to the tracks for approximately 6 kilometers, until you reach a road with black trail markings (15335). Follow the black road for about 2 more kilometers to the riverbed of Nahal Mador. (The road marked in red is not passable for regular vehicles. You need a jeep to drive on it. The alternative is to go through the phosphate plant and drive along the road marked in black. This is not always possible as the guard at the gate won't always allow you through.)

The road to Nahal Mador offers beautiful views. The eastern layers of the Hatira Ridge, which conceal the Large Makhtesh, dive down toward the Zin Plain. A yellowish hill is attached to them in a strange way (geologists call it an "incongruity"). The Hebrew name of the hill, Givat Mador, preserves the sound of the Bedouin name, al-Madriyya. This is a typical Negev table mountain – left over from strata of rock that once covered the Zin Plain and even the Hatira Ridge.

The slopes of the hill are composed of soft, yellowish marl and chalk of the Ghareb Formation, which contains the phosphates. The top of the hill is made of harder chalk, which gives it the shape of a table. As Nahal Zin dug its way through, the rocks of the Ghareb Formation were

Water holes in Nahal Afran.

swept from the mountainous areas and the remnants were left in the syncline of Nahal Zin.

Park the car east of Givat Mador, at the junction of a blue trail and a red trail. From here start hiking up Nahal Mador along the blue trail (15230).

To the Makhtesh Wall

If you are hiking in winter (February and March), the riverbed will be covered with flowers. The orange-flowered field marigolds (*Calendula arvensis*, or *tzipornei hatul metzuyot* – "common cat's-claws" – in Hebrew) will fill up the riverbed. This plant grows almost everywhere in Israel, except for the most remote recesses of the desert. The Roman squill (*Bellevalia desertorum*, or *zamzumit hamidbar*), with its blue flowers, will be another beauty.

After walking for 45 minutes, you will

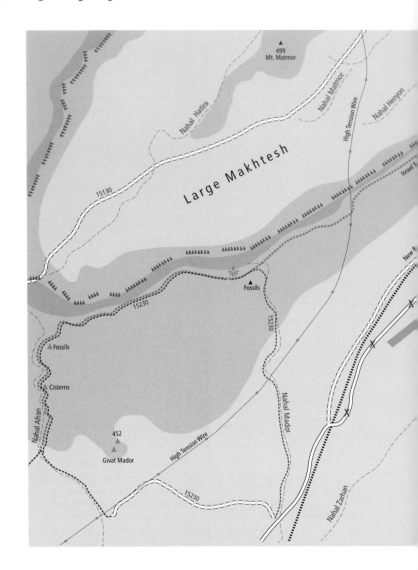

Mt. Matmor
499

Nahal Hatira

Nahal Matmor

Nahal Heryon

High Tension Wire

Large Makhtesh

Israel T

15130

15230

Fossils

15230

Fossils

New R

Cisterns

Nahal Afran

Nahal Mador

452

Givat Mador

High Tension Wire

15230

Nahal Zarhan

To Dimona

Oron

Phosphate
Plant

...t Road

To Nahal Zin

▲
465
Mt. Rechev

N

km

0   1   2

reach the slopes of the Hatira Ridge. The trail makes its way down several small falls, and wisely circumvents a larger fall. The falls accentuate the sharp slope of the layers of the Hatira Ridge on its eastern side. Sometimes they seem almost vertical. This is a beautiful segment of the trail.

After a total of an hour and a half of walking, you will come upon the Israel Trail. The trail passes along a huge wall with fossils of oysters of the genus Exogyra. These fossils are not rare, but the concentration of them here is impressive. Exogyra oysters inhabited a shallow marine area and they were very common in the Lower Cretaceous period (140-100 million years ago).

Here, on the shaded slopes, in the fissures of the rock, grow the round leaves of the common pennywort (*Umbilicus intermedius*, or *taborit netuyah* in Hebrew), a thoroughly Mediterranean plant. Shaded rock fissures are a Negev highlands habitat that sometimes provides shelter to plants that are not native to the desert. This phenomenon is due mainly to the fact that the pocket of ground in the fissure of the rock receives relatively large quantities of rainwater, which flows into it from the surrounding rock. At elevation point 682, the trail's marking changes its color to red. You are now at the top of Har Karbolet (Mt. Coxcomb). Such a name is not given to just any mountain, and indeed, the view is incredible. On one side, sprawls the Large Makhtesh. On the other side, are the sloped layers of the wall of the makhtesh. The trail runs along the "razor edge" in between, alternately descending and ascending, justifying the name given to it.

Far away from us in the south, Mt. Rechev on the Hatzera Ridge, the home of the Small Makhtesh, cam be seen. Further away is the Mahmal Ridge, which contains Makhtesh Ramon. The trail cuts across a deep riverbed and rises to the slope behind it, traversing a huge rock surface that is composed entirely of an immense concentration of Exogyra fossils. Then the trail leads down to Nahal Afran.

Nahal Afran

Nahal Afran is the highlight of this hike. Its name derives from the Bedouin name of the riverbed, Wadi Afran (the Riverbed on the Soil). The riverbed begins with a series of five rock cavities, which, in winter, fill with water. The slope with the cavities descends to a clear geological fault line. The inclined layers of this slope are simply swallowed up under a vertical layer of rock.

The layers of rock create quite a commotion here, twisting and turning in all kinds of whimsical ways. The trail runs steeply along the slanted layers, in narrow crevices. You have to walk slowly and carefully. Fast walking can easily end in a sprained ankle. Thus you pass from "crust" to "crust" of the makhtesh wall

until you reach the large waterfall. Here, too, the trail "breaks," circumventing the waterfall from the left with the aid of hand rungs.

The trail leaves the channel to avoid a group of boulders, ascends steeply, and leads back down to it in a very steep descent. Then you somehow pass between and under large boulders.

In the last "crust" of the Hatira Ridge, to the right of the trail, is a lovely group of packed fossils of tower snails. They are of the genus Cerithium; snails of that genus inhabited shallow seawater in the distant past. They are up to 7 centimeters long and their whorls are very prominent.

You now emerge from the belly of the mountain to the open landscape of the syncline that separates the Hatira and Hatzera anticlines. Nahal Afran digs through the sediments of the syncline on its way to its meeting with Nahal Mador.

The walk to the car along the red-marked trail (which has turned into a jeep track) is another 6 kilometers. (Desert savvy hikers can pre-arrange for the car to meet them close to the exit of Nahal Afran, thereby saving themselves a walk of an hour and a half.)

At the top of Mt. Karbolet.

Route 30:

Across Makhtesh Ramon

This hike follows the Israel Trail across the grand Makhtesh Ramon, from the Ramon Tooth, via the Carpenter's Shop to Mitzpe Ramon.

Route length: 12 km.
Difficulty: Easy to moderate.
Start point: Kilometer marker 84 on Route 40.
Access: From Mitzpe Ramon.
End point: Mitzpe Ramon.
Duration: 4-5 hours.
Admission fees: None.
Opening hours: None.
Equipment: Regular.
Remarks: None.
Pickup point for cars: Mitzpe Ramon Visitors' Center.
Map: Western Negev Highlands Hiking and Trail Map (18).

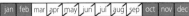

jan | feb | mar | apr | may | jun | jul | aug | sep | oct | nov | dec

To get to the beginning of the route, take Route 40 from Mitzpe Ramon down towards Eilat. Cross the makhtesh and exit it from the southern side. About 100 meters after kilometer marker 84 is a small parking area with a sign pointing to the Ammonite Wall. This is the beginning of our hike.

The Ramon Tooth

Follow the red-marked trail and the Israel Trail to the Ammonite Wall, which is a few hundred meters from the road. The Ammonites are large sea fossils that look like the ram's ears of the Egyptian god Amon. The wall has thousands of these large fossils stuck in it. (Do not take any!)

The red trail (18201) continues west to a bend in Nahal Nekarot. Here it makes a sharp turn to the right and starts to climb towards the Ramon Tooth (Shen Ramon in Hebrew). The tooth is a granite outcrop that towers over the southern wall of the makhtesh. The trail climbs up through black and red granite. The summit offers an amazing view of the makhtesh.

Continue down the northern slope of the tooth into the rounded hills that surround Nahal Ra'af. Gypsum abounds in this area and the holes in the ground and tracks seemingly leading nowhere are the remains of gypsum surveys and attempted quarrying.

The wells of Borot Ra'af are difficult to find mainly because they are dry and are really just a few depressions in the ground. The red trail continues down Nahal Ra'af to Nahal Ramon, the main river that drains the makhtesh.

On the other side of Nahal Ramon, the trail climbs towards the "Carpenter's Shop" — a hill covered with "baked" stones that turned into prisms. When the prisms fall from the rock, they create piles of stones that look like wooden beams. There are a few prism hills like this in the makhtesh, which are evidence that volcanic outflows that baked the sandstone hills created this phenomena. A small volcanic crater in the makhtesh attests to this activity.

From the prisms the trail, which has now turned green (18202), climbs up the cliff face to Mitzpe Ramon, reaching the Mitzpe Ramon crater promenade a little west of the town. From here, you can walk down the promenade to the east (right) and reach the visitors' center, or follow the promenade to the west (left) to camel hill — a hump-like hill which is a favorite Mitzpe Ramon site for watching the sunset.

Route 31:
Rhubarb on the Rocks

Rare plants, glorious panoramas, and intriguing basalt prisms are among the treats to be found on a hike in the western Negev highlands.

Route length: 22 km.
Difficulty: The route is relatively easy. You have to cover a height differential of some 200 meters twice going down and twice coming up.
Start point: Kilometer marker 12 on Route 171.
Access: From Mitzpe Ramon.
End point: Arod Pass Road.
Duration: 8 hours.
Admission fees: None.
Opening hours: None.
Equipment: Regular.
Remarks: This trip should not be attempted in the summer. Do not leave your car unattended in the area – car thieves abound.
Pickup point for cars: Arrange to be picked up at the junction of the Arod Pass Road (marked in blue) with Nahal Lotz (marked in red). Any vehicle can reach the pickup point.
Map: Western Negev Highlands Hiking and Trail Map (No. 18).

| jan | feb | mar | apr | may | jun | jul | aug | sep | oct | nov | dec |

To get to the beginning of the trail, drive westward from Mitzpe Ramon on the road that leads to Mt. Harif (Route 171) to the small parking lot, beside kilometer marker 12. From here, follow the green trail (18260) southward. The trail climbs up a shallow riverbed that drains the gentle northern slope of the Ramon Ridge into the riverbed of Nahal Nitzana. Like many riverbeds of its kind, it is covered densely with desert shrubs such as white wormwood and jointed anabasis.

The abundant vegetation and the remains of agricultural terraces attest to the extensive agriculture that existed here in the Byzantine period. Every shallow gorge was cultivated. The cultivation improved the condition of the soil in the riverbeds and now they are filled with desert plants that "remember" ancient times.

The vegetation in the riverbed is the main means of sustenance for the herbivorous animals that inhabit this area. Gazelles and ibexes have been here from time immemorial and in 1984 the INPA reintroduced herds of onagers to the Israeli wild in Makhtesh Ramon. The onagers are doing well, have reproduced nicely, and can now be found throughout the large expanse between Nahal Tzihur and the Barnea Plateau (beside Shivta). The Negev highlands has a "resident" herd numbering about 30 onagers. It makes do with food that nature offers, but is aided by a water trough installed by the INPA. Onager tracks and droppings can be seen in abundance in this area. The length of a mature onager's hoof is 6 or 7 centimeters.

The only animals around that don't belong to the reserve are camels, used by

Basalt rocks in the Canyon of the Prisms.

smugglers bringing goods from Egypt to the southern part of Mt. Hebron.

Down into Makhtesh Ramon

The green trail meets up with a trail marked in blue, which continues to the right. Don't turn onto it, but continue along the green trail to the rim of Makhtesh Ramon. When you get to the rim, make a little detour to the right, to a wall built beneath a long rock shelf. In the past, shepherds used to take shelter in the chamber that is formed by the wall.

Here, some 200 meters above the makhtesh floor, the view is breathtaking. The entire length of the makhtesh can be seen, all the way up to the Mahmal Valley, Mt. Ardon, and the Ardon Valley. Mitzpe Ramon can be made out on the northern cliff of the makhtesh, and also Mt. Arod, a mass of black basalt rising some 230 meters from the makhtesh floor.

Now follow the trail down to the makhtesh floor; the ancient trail meanders gently, its stones cleared away long ago to create a passage for heavily laden camels. On the makhtesh floor, the trail turns eastward, toward basalt hills, and enters a small basalt crevice, known as the Canyon of the Prisms. The crevice's walls reveal beautiful exposures of basalt prisms, toothed peaks, and dark split rock arrayed in little columns. The prisms incline slightly to the west, a phenomenon that seems to indicate that the prisms formed during the flow of lava. In any event, it's a delightful place to stop for breakfast.

After exiting the Canyon of the Prisms and entering the expanses of the makhtesh, the trail meets up with a black-marked dirt road (18240) that runs beside Nahal Ramon, the riverbed that drains Makhtesh Ramon. Walk westward (right) along the road for nearly 2 kilometers, until you arrive at a junction with a trail that is marked in red (18232) and which climbs southward (to the left) and leads up the southern cliff of the makhtesh.

Leaving the Makhtesh

The southern cliff of the makhtesh rises some 150 meters above the makhtesh floor. Still, it's not a bad climb, especially since it takes you past red and purple sandstone rocks from the Lower Cretaceous epoch (144 million years ago).

Moreover, in winter the slope is festooned with wild rhubarb, a plant rare in Israel that grows only in the western part of Makhtesh Ramon and in the Nahal Arod area, from a height of 700 meters and up. Each plant develops up to three large leaves, whose diameter, after particularly rainy winters, can be as much as 70 centimeters — a very strange sight in the desert. In spring, the plant blossoms with red flowers. When summer begins, the leaves fall off and the plant endures the heat as a thickened root sheltered deep in the ground.

Once up the cliff, the trail runs along a razor edge range, which marks the peak of the vertical layers of the southern slope of the Ramon Ridge. Prior to the erosive activity that formed the makhtesh, these layers climbed up to the top of the Ramon Ridge. The trail leaves the edge of the makhtesh with a sharp turn to the right, heading in the direction of Mt. Ido, which is about 1 kilometer away.

At the top of Mt. Karbolet.

Atlantic pistachio tree.

A trail with a "transparent" marking (whose two white stripes flank an unpainted space rather than the usual colored stripe) branches off from the red trail and climbs to the top of Mt. Ido (959 meters). Mt. Ido is a table mountain, consisting of surviving rock from a plateau that underwent erosion and geological upheaval. It is composed of white limestone from the Eocene epoch, about 58 million years ago.

The view from the top is amazing. The northern cliff of Makhtesh Ramon, Mt. Ramon, Mt. Harif to the north, Mt. Arif, which contains two makhteshim, and rising behind it, Mt. Karkom, which is famous for its rock drawings to the south.

Looking east, you can see Mt. Tzuri'az,

Mt. Tzenifim, and all the way to Mt. Edom. To the west, are the Lotz Cliffs, which is where we are headed.

To the Lotz Cliffs

From the top of Mt. Ido, the red trail descends to Nahal Arod, crosses the riverbed, and reaches a dirt road (marked in blue, 18270) that runs along the riverbed. Turn right on the blue road and pass a campsite. Here, too, many wild rhubarbs can be seen in winter.

Not far from the campsite, grow a few Atlantic pistachio trees. Several hundred Atlantic pistachios have survived in the Negev highlands. They are centuries old and a few of them are huge, especially the ones that grow in large riverbeds, such as Nahal Arod and Nahal Lotz, which collect sizable amounts of water. Others grow in rock fissures. They are smaller, but no less endowed with the hardiness that enables them to continue to survive in the harsh conditions of the Negev highlands.

After a walk of nearly 2 kilometers on Nahal Arod's blue-marked dirt road, a junction with a trail marked in black is reached. Turn south (left) onto this trail (18370), which leads up a little riverbed. The trail ascends gently to the top of the Lotz Cliffs. In addition to the large white broom bushes that prevail in the area, there are two big shrubs. One of them is bladder senna, which has large yellow flowers. The other is *Rhamnus disperma*, a densely tangled shrub with pointy branches. In Israel, this plant can be found growing in the Negev highlands and in the southern part of the Judean Desert.

The trail reaches the top of the Lotz Ascent, another lovely lookout point with a view of Mt. Batur and the Hisun Valley; the high plateaus of Mt. Nes and Mt. Sagi, Mt. Haspas, with Mt. Karkom rising behind it; and Mt. Arif. Also visible is the canyon of Nahal Ketziya, which drains into Nahal Arod and the Barak Plateau. From the top of the Lotz Ascent, follow the green-marked trail (18371) leading to Nahal Eliav. The landscape is similar to the landscape in which you ascended, but the Atlantic pistachios here are larger.

In spring, the yellow asphodel and the *Tulipa systola* (*tzvoni hamidbar* – "desert tulips" – in Hebrew) flower here together with the *Ferula daninii* (*kelach danin* – "Danin fennel" – in Hebrew), a plant

Canyon of the Prisms.

known for its cuplike appearance and endemic to the western Negev highlands and the Sde Boker area.

In addition, if you are lucky, you might spot a sand rat, a creature that can be as large as 17 centimeters long.

The green trail leads down Nahal Eliav. But this time turn off at the black trail (18372) leading off to the right and up a small ridge and down into Nahal Lotz, which has a red-marked jeep track running through it (18374). Turn right at the jeep track and walk for 300 meters to the meeting point with the excellent dirt road (marked in blue, 18210) passable to any vehicle. This is the place that your driver should be waiting to pick you up.

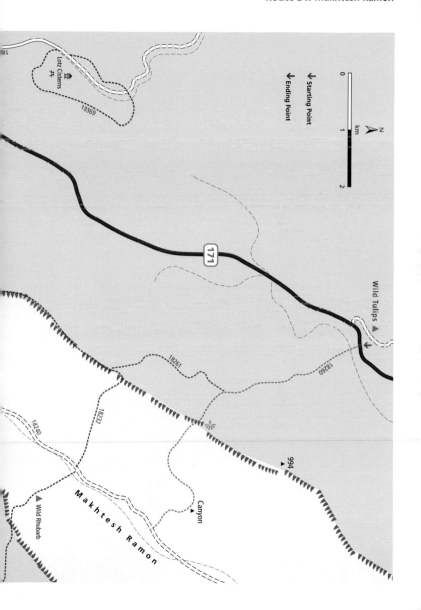

Route 32:
Smugglers' Pass

A challenging two-day hike across the Negev Highlands to the Wells of Oded, Mt. Arif, and Mt. Karkom – all candidates for the biblical Mountain of the Lord.

Route length: First day – 11 km, 7 hours. Second day – 20 km, 11 hours.

Difficulty: For good hikers.

Start point: Oded Wells.

Access: Access to the starting point, to campsites, and the end point of the trip is by 4x4 only.

End point: Mount Karkom Campsite.

Duration: First day, 7 hours. Second day, 11 hours.

Admission fees: None.

Opening hours: None.

Equipment: Do not rely on finding water sources on the route. Bring sufficient water for both days.

Remarks: The hike takes place in an active military firing zone. It is absolutely prohibited to set out for a hike without coordinating it with the army, even on Saturdays and holidays. Tel. (08) 990-2927.

Campsites: First night – campsite north of the Wells of Oded, or any other authorized site in the Negev. Second night – campsite at the western foot of Mt. Arif.

Pickup point for cars: Access and pickup by jeep.

Map: Western Negev Highlands Hiking and Trail Map (No. 18).

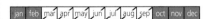

jan | feb | mar | apr | may | jun | jul | aug | sep | oct | nov | dec

To get to the starting point, take a jeep along Route 171 to the turnoff to the Arod Ascent, between kilometer markers 5 and 6. Take the blue-marked unpaved road (18210) to the Arod Ascent, for a view of Makhtesh Ramon. From here on, travel is by jeep only. Descend the Arod Ascent, on the blue-marked track, passing several beautiful Atlantic pistachio trees. Continue to the junction with the track marked in green (18340) that leads to the Wells of Oded. This is a better way to get to the wells than the track marked in black.

Be'erot Oded (the Wells of Oded) is the name of a group of ancient wells of unknown age dug in an alluvial terrace of the riverbed of Nahal Arod. Among the large saltbushes, six wells can be found; their openings are made of several courses of stones. Each of them contained water about 5 meters deep.

South of the wells is a large concentration of Bedouin graves. Desert nomads have always preferred to bury their dead at crossroads and other central spots, apparently in order to facilitate pilgrimage to and protection of the graves. In this cemetery, each grave is marked with a large pile of stones, surrounded by a frame of larger stones. The graves are all oriented in the same direction — in Islamic burial, the aim is to place the body in such a way that the the face of the deceased will be facing toward Mecca. This graveyard conforms to that practice.

On the Way to Mt. Arif

Start the hike with the trail, marked in green (18340), that leads away from the wells through a small riverbed. The limestone rock is white and polished by the water that flows through it when it rains. Between the benchlike masses of rock grow large bushes of white broom (*Retama raetam*, or *rotem hamidbar* in Hebrew).

The trail, winding along an S-like curve, leads up to a plateau. To the north, the Mahmal Ridge comes into view, with its geological layers exposed. To the south, Mt. Arif is already visible. The trail leads down a wide riverbed with additional graves on its periphery, reaching — after a short distance — the large riverbed of Nahal Ketzia, which, further on, cuts through the strata of Mt. Arif.

Here and there, snack-food wrappers and plastic milk sacks are strewn along the trail; they were left by smugglers from Egypt, judging by the printing on the wrappers. The smugglers, like obedient hikers, made sure to stick to the marked trails, even if they did leave a lot of litter behind. The trail winds a little down Nahal Ketzia before heading south, up the slopes of Mt. Arif. Before ascending the mountain, the trail leads into a deep gorge that leads into Nahal Ketzia, and then climbs up the banks of the canyon to the top of Mt. Arif.

Two Makhteshim for the Price of One

The climb to the summit is a short one. The green trail reaches the watershed of the Arif Ridge. Here, at the point it meets up with a blue trail that leads up to the summit (959 meters), the summit is adorned with a pile of stones with a metal pole in the center that is used as a reference point by surveyors. Some 30 meters further east is a rock shelf that affords the best view.

Cliff on the way to Mt. Karkom.

The view from Mt. Arif is simply heart-stopping. In the distance you see the Mahmal Ridge, containing Makhtesh Ramon. Mitzpeh Ramon rises at the top of the cliff. The riverbeds of Nahal Karkom and Nahal Arod meander between the hills that remained in the synclines (troughs of stratified rock) surrounding the ridge. You can also see Mt. Sagi and Mt. Karkom. Especially beautiful is the view of the gigantic Meishar Plain. Above it rises the wall of the Arif cliffs and the Hadav Plateau, which mark the continuation of the anticline to which Mt. Arif belongs. Peeking out on the far horizon, in Sinai, is the top of Mt. Arif A-Naka, which is also the continuation of our anticline. The Mountains of Edom also loom on the horizon.

Mt. Arif's northwestern slope rises gently from the Arod-Nekarot riverbed systems. From the other side, the slope is very steep, dropping at an angle of more than 50°. Between these slopes lie two deep makhteshim; they look like they are eroding right before your eyes. They are much smaller than their big brothers — Makhtesh Ramon, the Small Makhtesh, and the Large Makhtesh. The northern one of them is about 1,200 meters long and about 500 meters wide. The southern one is about 2.5 kilometers long and up to 600 meters wide. From the summit of Mt. Arif, you can see nearly every meter.

Both of the makhteshim are about 200 meters deep. Like the other Negev makhteshim, the Mt. Arif makhteshim have breaches in their eastern walls through which riverbeds pass on their way to the Arava. These makhteshim, too, have colorful sandstone exposures. Unfortunately, there is no marked trail leading into them and so entry is permitted only with special authorization from the INPA.

Descend along the western slopes of the mountain along the blue trail (18440) to reach the campsite, which is just a flat surface situated in a little valley, relatively sheltered from the wind at the junction of the blue trail and a red track (18360). Your jeep should meet you here after taking the red track along Nahal Ma'azar.

The Enchanted Riverbed

In the morning, your jeep should take you 4 km further south, along the track that is marked in black on the map (it is not a marked trail!), to the beginning of the black trail linking Mt. Arif with Mt. Karkom

(18445). This trail was marked at the initiative of Amitai Merkin, who was a Negev Highlands ranger for the INPA. Merkin convinced the biologists of the INPA that it was possible to mark the trail to Mt. Karkom and expose this unknown portion of the Negev to visitors. (Merkin was killed in a helicopter accident beside Mt. Arbel when he was spreading food containing rabies vaccines for wild animals.) The meticulous and consistent marking enables the hiker to walk along this untamed route without fear of going astray.

The trail begins on a plateau and enters a little gorge. Looking back at Mt. Arif, you can now see it in all its splendor. The trail descends to a tributary of Nahal Beruka. The landscape here, with ridges popping up at the bends in the riverbed, is reminiscent of the topography of the Judean mountains.

Opposite you is the large and beautiful mass of Mt. Haspas, one of the points along the Paran Rift, a vast geological fault that continues from central Sinai, crosses the width of the Negev, and reaches the mountain of Kipat Eshet in the Arava. You don't have to be a professional geologist to discern that the rock of Mt. Haspas is very different from that of the ridge attached to it from the north.

At the foot of Mt. Haspas, beside a wall of yellow clay containing slabs of gypsum, the trail makes a sharp turn to the right. Follow it up to the western edge of Mt. Haspas. The trail then descends to the broad valley of Nahal Beruka, one of the large tributaries of Nahal Karkom. The riverbed narrows between the slopes of Mt. Haspas and Mt. Michael. The incline of

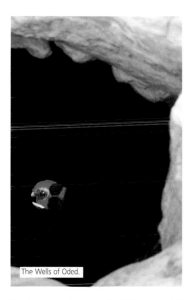
The Wells of Oded.

the layers creates an optical illusion and it is very difficult to know where the riverbed comes from and where it is going.

To Mt. Karkom

The trail emerges from Nahal Beruka and descends into Nahal Karkom. A short walk up the large riverbed of Nahal Karkom, one of the largest tributaries of Nahal Paran, brings you to Be'er Karkom (the Karkom Well) – a series of empty cisterns. A gigantic tamarisk grows in the largest one.

From Be'er Karkom, the trail ascends, via a network of shallow riverbeds and the remains of an ancient "neighborhood," on a steep ascent to elevation point 804. From here the trail runs along a razorlike ridge, with a lovely view. Huge rock crevices show the power of the erosive forces, acting here in combination with the Paran Rift. Because of the rift, the hard covering of the rock broke apart, exposing the soft rock that comprises Mt. Karkom.

Finally the trail reaches the final destination of this trip: Mt. Karkom, a large plateau covered with flint. Several marked trails (18536, 18537, 18538) lead the hiker among the thousands of ancient rock drawings, which are carved on nearly every protruding block of flint. These primitive drawings, mainly of ibexes and hunters, exist in many places in the Negev.

The rock drawings have aroused speculation that Mt. Karkom could be Mt. Sinai. If time permits (and remember you still have to drive out of the desert), the best thing to do is to take the blue trail (18536) to the look out point at its end, where the stones of the "temple" stand overlooking the vast expanses of the far Negev. Return along the green trail (18538), detouring to the huge dry waterfall, before climbing up the ridge and descending along the ancient ascent to the mountain to the foot of Mount Karkom, where your jeep should be waiting at the parking lot. To drive out of the area, take the red-marked track (18535) to Route 10 along the border with the Sinai.

One last remark: Visiting Mount Karkom can take two to three hours. You should consider camping out for another night at the foot of Mount Karkom and climbing it the next day. If this is your plan, take the black path (18537) up the mountain from the campsite, returning to the camp via the blue and green paths.

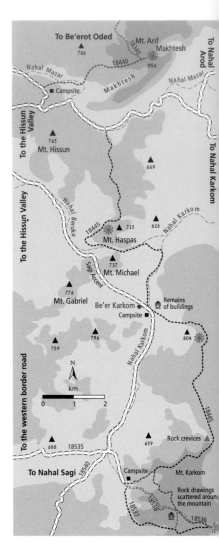

Rock drawings on Mt. Karkom.

View of the northern makhtesh.

Route 33:
Ada Canyon

A hike up a hidden canyon in the cliff face of Nahal Paran, the mightiest riverbed in the Negev. Ada's head, carved in the rock above the riverbed, is an added bonus.

Route length: 8 km.
Difficulty: Easy. 2 large ladders have to be climbed.
Start point: Kilometer marker 50 on Route 40.
Access: From Mitzpe Ramon.
End point: Ring route.
Duration: 3 hours.
Admission fees: None.
Opening hours: None.
Equipment: Regular and a short rope.
Remarks: A small waterfall has to be climbed, a rope can help. A rope and ladders in the canyon have to be negotiated. Bring a safety rope for children.
Pickup point for cars: End of route.
Map: Central Arava and Eastern Negev Highlands Hiking and Trail Map (No. 17).

jan | feb | mar | apr | may | jun | jul | aug | sep | oct | nov | dec

A cliff by Ada Canyon.

Ada Canyon.

Take Route 40 south from Mitzpe Ramon all the way to kilometer marker 50. The road descends into the wide riverbed of Nahal Paran, the longest and largest riverbed in the Negev. Nahal Paran is known for its large flash floods that can sweep everything out of their way – from cars trying to cross the river to trees, stones, and anything else in the riverbed. Never enter the river when it is flooded and never enter the river when there is a flash flood warning! (Flash flood warnings are broadcasted on the radio weather reports and can be obtained from the Israel Meteorological Service.) A few hundred meters after the kilometer marker, you will come to a pumping station on the left side of the road. Opposite it is a track marked in red (19160). Take the track (not the paved road!) to the right and drive to the riverbed of Nahal Paran. Jeeps and high vehicles can continue from here. Regular vehicles should park here (crossing the riverbed is tricky).

Up Nahal Paran

Walk along the track that leads up Nahal Paran. The track crosses the riverbed and runs along the bottom of the cliffs along the southern side of the river. Two kilometers later, the track starts to move away from the cliff, at a point where the cliffs make a sharp turn to the south. Keep walking along the bottom of the cliff until you come to a crack in the cliff with a path leading up it. (A sign on a pole marks the entrance, but after strong floods the sign has usually been washed away by the river.) You are now at the entrance to the Ada Canyon.

The Canyon

A blue trail leads up the canyon. The trail twists a little at the beginning, enters a gorge that keeps getting narrower and narrower as you continue, twisting and turning among the sandstone rock. At a certain point, it gets so narrow that it has to be negotiated sideways.

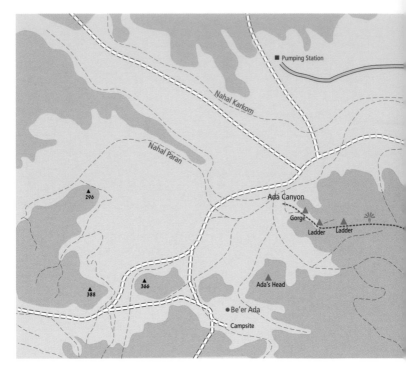

The narrow part of the canyon ends at a small dry waterfall. Some clever rock scrambling here will take you to the top of the waterfall (a rope is helpful to aid the less nimble of the group). Above the waterfall, the canyon opens up a little. Two more waterfalls have to be negotiated, this time with the aid of ladders and ropes that have been placed in the canyon. Once at the top, walk a little to the right to get to the edge of the cliff (hold on to the kids!!!).

From the cliff edge there is a wonderful view of the wide expanses of Nahal Paran and Nahal Karkom. Underneath you, in the small boxed valley, are the Ada Wells, a series of shallow wells dug into the riverbed to the water table. The wells are nearly always empty – but are a favorite camping site for jeeps on their way up Nahal Paran. On the cliff on the other side of the valley, Ada's head can be seen, carved out of the rock. This natural rock formation looks like a women with a high hairdo (it's a little like Marge Simpson's!).

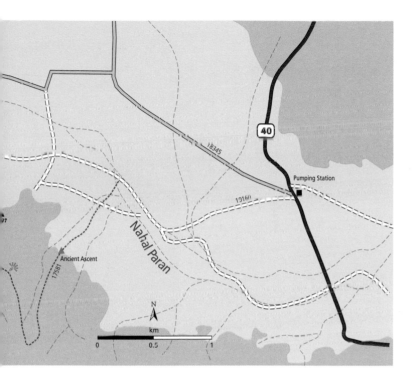

Now follow the blue-marked trail along the plateau. Every now and then, windows in the cliff face will open up affording a good view from the top of the cliff that you walked along to reach the canyon.

After walking for 15 minutes, the trail makes a turn to the right leading toward elevation point 409. Here it meets up with an ancient camel track. The trail makes a U-turn to the left and now follows the camel track all the way to an ancient ascent that descends down to the riverbed of Nahal

Paran, a few hundred meters from where you left the car. Turn right on the red-marked track and walk back to the car.

One last warning. Technically, the trail is inside a military firing zone, inside the safety perimeter. The army does not train on the weekends, so jeep tours and hikers often travel through the area on weekends and holidays without coordinating their trips with the army in advance. That said, if you want to be "legally perfect," you should coordinate your trip with the army.

Route 34:
Red, White, and Copper

Timna Park resembles a wonderland: steep mountains surround a desert valley that contains an artificial lake, ancient copper mines, multicolored sand, and trails that hikers of all ages and abilities can enjoy.

Route length: 2 km.
Difficulty: Suitable for families. There are ladders at several points on the trail.
Start point: Arches parking lot.
Access: From Route 90, south of Yotvata, follow signs pointing west to the park entrance.
End point: Arches parking lot.
Duration: 2 hours.
Admission fees: Admission charge to Timna Park.
Opening hours: Sat.-Thurs.: 8 a.m. - 4 p.m. Fri. and holiday eves until 2 p.m.
Equipment: Regular.
Remarks: Timna Park contains about 20 trails that lead to attractions such as Solomon's Pillars, the Shrine of Hathor, and the Mushroom. There are children's activities near the lake, a multimedia presentation at the entrance, and a Bedouin tent in which coffee, tea, and light meals are available. www.timna-park.co.il
Pickup point for cars: End of route.
Map: Timna Park Map (available at park gate).

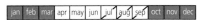

| jan | feb | mar | apr | may | jun | jul | aug | sep | oct | nov | dec |

The Mushroom at Timna Park.

Timna Park, located some 30 kilometers north of Eilat, is action-packed, with additions to the natural attractions added every year. It could be a stunning multimedia presentation or a night time hike to view Solomon's Pillars, the Mushroom, or other dramatically illuminated attractions. One of the latest innovation is the Light and Copper Tour, a night-time tour that allows visitors to observe lights, shadows, and images flickering over the park's rocks. New hiking trails have also been set up thanks to the creative imagination of Michael (Levko) Lavi, the park's director. One of our favorite trails has the unimaginative name of "1A, Short Route." But don't let the name deter you – this isn't just another trail.

The Trail

In the Arches parking lot (number 22 on the Timna Park maps), next to the colorful sculpture of the Egyptian god Horus, a flight of stairs with red trail markings is carved into the white sandstone. This beautiful white sandstone crumbles into white sand, which carpets the small valley around the parking lot. From here, you can see the back of the Small Arch, an impressive five-meter-high "window" in the red sandstone. Head for the arch, reaching it via a climb up a metal ladder, and then stop to enjoy the colorful view of the Edom Mountains, Hachlil Mountain, Timna Mountain, and the Timna Valley and the enclosing mountains that protect it like a shield.

A trail with green markings leads downward through a very narrow crevice to an open, sand-covered valley. Turn right, following a red-marked trail, and pass the Crack, a deep, very narrow fissure in the rock that is home to nesting rock doves.

The sand-covered valleys look beautiful, not just because of their colors, but also because of the absence of plant life that turns them into a kind of moonscape. The meager rainfall – an average of 15 mm a year – isn't sufficient to allow plants to grow among the rocks. The plants grow mainly in the riverbeds, subsisting on the water that runs down from the rocks around. All this makes the tiny acacia growing in the small gorge further down the path even more noteworthy. In spite of its advanced age, it isn't even a meter tall because it doesn't receive enough water to sustain further growth. This acacia's mere existence is a biological miracle.

The next interesting attraction is the Egyptian Mining Cave. The park staff has set up a sculpture by it of an Egyptian miner at work. From the twelfth to the fourteenth century BCE, during the New Kingdom in Egypt, the pharaohs sent delegations of workers to mine copper at Timna. They set up a huge copper production industry, apparently with the assistance of Midianite experts from Edom. They dug deep shafts – digging as much as 40 meters into the rock – in order to reach the rich copper ores. The shafts were connected to one another, creating a many-branched network of caves.

In the mining caves, follow the black trail markings and climb up the comfortable peg ladder to the top of a 24-meter-long shaft. At the top of the shaft is a red sandstone platform from which there is a great view of the Timna Valley and the Edom Mountains.

The view of Timna Valley.

Not far from here is a network of mining caves from the Chalcolithic period (some 5,000 years ago). This was the period when humans in this area made the jump from using only stone tools to fashioning tools out of copper. During this period, the miners only managed to dig shafts that were three to five meters deep. They uncovered copper ores and pounded them with stone hammers.

Even today it is easy to differentiate between the Chalcolithic and Egyptian mines. The Egyptian miners worked with bronze chisels, which left sharp, precise marks on the rock. The stone hammers that the miners of the Chalcolithic period used left blunt marks on the mine walls. This can be seen clearly further along the trail, next to the small riverbed in which a Chalcolithic mine intersects with an Egyptian one.

Our trail ends at the network of caves from the Chalcolithic period. Enter the caves from the one side and walk out through the opposite side. It is an easy walk, even though taller people will have to crouch. The mine features a sculpture of an ancient miner, complete with a stone hammer and a basket, which he used to remove copper dust from the mine and bring it to the smelting works.

The short corridor that leads back to the parking lot is completely covered with small grains of copper, which are scattered throughout the area. Humans began collecting the copper grains at Timna at the end of the Stone Age, some 6,000 years ago. At the time, they didn't know how to turn copper into tools, but they used it to fashion jewelry, which it is still used for today. This thought brings us full circle on a trail that leads through 6,000 years of history.

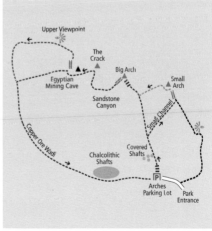

Route 35:
Enjoying the Hue

The hike from Mt. Neshef to Nahal Zfunot is probably the most colorful walk in Israel. It begins in the black hills of Mt. Neshef, continues in the red rock of Nahal Shani, and ends in the frenzy of colors of the sandstone in Nahal Zfunot.

Route length: 16 km (not including Nahal Shlalgon).
Difficulty: For proficient hikers.
Start point: Mt. Neshef. The trail to the mountain (marked in blue) begins from the approach road to the Mt. Uzziah army base, which turns off from the Western Border Road (Route 12) about 2 km south of the approach road to the Red Canyon.
Access: Western Border Road (Route 12).
End point: The parking lot beside the seismographic station in the Arava. Access to the station is via a paved road that turns off west from the Arava Road (Route 90), between kilometer markers 24 and 25.
Duration: 8-9 hours.
Admission fees: None.
Opening hours: None.
Equipment: Regular.
Remarks: There is no drinking water along the route. Come equipped with a sufficient quantity.
Pickup point for cars: End of route.
Map: Eilat Mountains Hiking and Trail Map (No. 20, English edition).

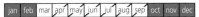

jan feb mar apr may jun jul aug sep oct nov dec

This hike begins, admittedly, in a way that is not very encouraging. The trail marked in blue (20375), the one climbing to the dark summit of Mt. Neshef from the approach road to the Mt. Uzziah army base, not only looks steep – it really is steep.

Still, it's not too bad. And after only 25 minutes you can already stand on Mt. Neshef (863 meters above sea level) and enjoy the fabulous view of the riverbed of Nahal Shani, through which the famous Red Canyon runs, almost at your feet. To your south, the sharp peaks of the Eilat Mountains can be seen.

The view to the west is particularly interesting. It reveals that Mt. Neshef is the eastern edge of a long ridge, whose peaks – Jabel Karayn Atud and Jabel el-Hamra (called the Red Mountain in Hebrew) – rise from the Moon Valley in Sinai. The dark-hued Mt. Neshef is different from most of the Eilat Mountains, a fact that requires a brief geological explanation.

Most of the Eilat Mountains are made of plutonic rock, which formed from the slow solidification of magma in the depth of the earth's crust. This rock, whose most conspicuous representative is granite, is made of large crystals. It is hard rock, which creates a cliffy landscape. Mt. Neshef, on the other hand, is made of rhyolite, rock that was formed by magma that burst out of the earth. The chemical composition of rhyolite resembles that of granite, but it is made of tiny crystals that form rock that is less resistant to erosion. The result: Mt. Neshef eroded relatively quickly and therefore it is dome-shaped. The crumbling rock makes the mountain soft and somewhat serrated.

In Hebrew, *neshef* means evening or night. The mountain's name was derived from the dark color of its rock. Indeed, in your ascent to the top of the mountain, you might recall this biblical verse: "Give glory to the Lord your God, before He cause darkness, and before your feet stumble upon the dark mountains" (Jer. 13:16)

Going down, everything is a lot easier. The trail descends northward in a little ravine, in a landscape that is very much like the mountains of Sinai, and reaches a broad riverbed, in which you will find a lovely row of acacia trees – of the species known as *Acacia gerrardii*, or *shitat hanegev* (Negev acacia in Hebrew).

On the Way to Nahal Shani

In Israel, the Negev acacia occupies the high areas between Nahal Paran and Eilat. Usually these trees are not found below a height of 500 meters above sea level, which proves that they can stand the cold better than their desert sisters. From a distance, they are identifiable by the grey tinge at the top. When you get closer, you can discern the giant thistles and the relatively large leaves, up to 7 millimeters long.

The rock of the Eilat Mountains is a habitat of the *Uromastyx ornatus*, or *hardonetzav hador* ("ornate tortoise-lizard") in Hebrew, a very large reptile that can grow to a length of 35 centimeters. The male's grey body is indeed ornate, adorned with yellow stripes and spots, its sides are green, and its head is blue. The female has a reddish body. Only lucky hikers get to see this rare creature.

The short riverbed with the acacias drains into a southern tributary of Nahal Shani, which is called by hikers and by the

The cliffs of Nahal Shani.

Further along, the riverbed becomes more tranquil and walking in it is easier and faster. Note the fact that the large acacias grow on the periphery of the channel since from time to time the riverbed is heavily flooded and all the vegetation in the center is uprooted.

A red-marked trail (20370) turns left and climbs up to Nahal Shlalgon, which subsequently returns to Nahal Raham. The channel of Nahal Shlalgon is monotonous, apart from clusters of fossils. You can, in good conscience, continue down Nahal Shani until it meets up with Nahal Raham, and do without a visit to Nahal Shlalgon.

Nahal Raham

Nahal Raham, one of the longest riverbeds of the Eilat Mountains, drains an area of some 100 square kilometers. The riverbed begins south of Mt. Uzziah and descends to the Arava. You meet it in the middle and turn south (right, black trail 20458), upward. In a few minutes, you are greeted by the sloping facade of a large rock surface. Here, the riverbed bursts out of a narrow gorge dotted with pits. This place is known as the Raham water holes, though these pits fill up with water only once in a great while. Walking along the nearly invisible shallow steps hewn on the little rock waterfall makes the climb easier.

official signs "Southern Nahal Shani." The trail passes here between colorful rock shoulders, reaches the top of a large waterfall, about 30 meters high, and circumvents the waterfall from the right in a steep descent. At the bottom is a shady canyon, which digs through red and white sandstone and is definitely a good place for a breakfast break.

The Southern Shani (follow the black markings, 20372) continues in a beautiful canyon, between erect sandstone cliffs, until it reaches the broad channel of Nahal Shani (green markings, 20371). The beginning of the riverbed becomes a large canyon and the trail passes among big rocks that have fallen into the channel. The banks are composed alternately of colorful sandstone and limestone from layers of the plateau above the riverbed that have "fallen" down here.

Approximately 400 meters beyond the pits, the riverbed widens into a small valley. Two small groups of palm trees grow among the acacia trees. The palms in one cluster are tiny and unimpressive, but the second group includes three nice, large shade-giving trees. The palms subsist here on the valley's high underground water,

Trail markings in the desert.

which is almost at surface level. Veteran hikers have often seen ibexes digging for drinking water here.

The serene valley is a wonderful place for another break. You can sit in the shade and watch the scrub warblers hopping around. The scrub warbler is a kind of grey desert warbler, with a darker tail, which it raises up. Its nest is a large structure with an opening from the side, built among the branches of a shrub.

The Amram Ascent and Nahal Zfunot

From the Raham palms, the trail (blue, 20460) leads up a gentle slope to a trail marked in red (20430). Turn left on the red trail to reach Mitzpe Amram (the Amram Lookout Point), 638 meters above sea level. Here, suddenly, there is a fabulous view, one

of the most breathtaking in the Eilat Mountains: the Arava Valley, the Mountains of Edom, the Gulf of Eilat, Har Shlomo (Mt. Solomon), the Nahal Raham basin, the Neshef mountains, and the Timna Cliffs. At your feet are the marvelous landscapes of a valley that can be called Makhtesh Amram.

The lookout point is at the top of a cliff that surrounds Makhtesh Amram, 400 meters above its floor. The boundaries of the makhtesh are distinct, with a belt of high cliffs around it: in the north, the Evrona cliffs; in the west, the cliff of Puah Hill; in the south, the cliff of Mt. Amir. In the east, toward the Arava Plain, the cliff is completely broken open, though it is possible to see a small limestone hump beside the road, the remnant of the eroded cliff.

Makhtesh Amram is very similar in shape to the famous makhteshim of the Negev highlands. Here, too, the surrounding cliffs are made of colored sandstone at the bottom and layers of hard limestone above. However, in Makhtesh Amram, the rock is much older. Protruding from the floor is Amram Hill, a large, black volcanic massif from the Precambrian era (more than 545 million years ago) that apparently rose and broke through the surface. In this makhtesh, layers of sandstone from the Paleozoic era (545-230 million years ago) are exposed, and also sandstone and limestone layers that are known from the Negev makhteshim. The layers of sandstone and limestone around the core of the volcanic massif eroded and formed a round valley that is completely closed. The sinking of the Arava Valley in the east opened the wall of the eastern cliff.

The red-marked trail continues on the high periphery that encircles Makhtesh Amram. Every step that you take exposes new forms and colors and provides a different perspective. After 2 kilometers, the trail leaves the perimeter of the cliff and descends northward in a steep riverbed to Nahal Zfunot — one of the most beautiful riverbeds in the Eilat Mountains. The riverbed first cuts crevices in the white sandstone and then a fantastic canyon in red sandstone, creating a feast for the eyes. The narrow canyon widens into a broad valley, called the "Hidden Valley." At the junction with the black trail, turn left and follow the black trail up a short ascent. At the top, you descend to a fenced area in which there is a seismographic station. Here, at the end of the paved road that branches off from the Arava Road, you conclude what is probably the most colorful hike you can take in Israel.

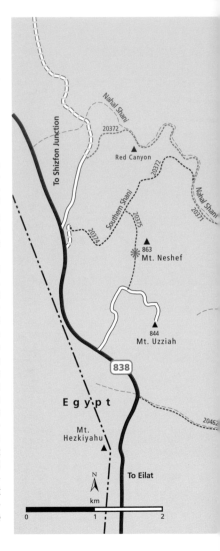

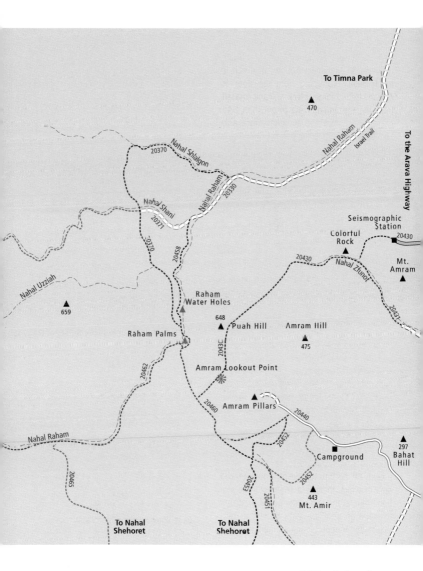

To Timna Park

▲ 470

Nahal Shalgon
20370

Nahal Raham

20330

Nahal Shani

20371

20370

20458

Nahal Uzziah

▲ 659

Israel Trail

Nahal Raham

Seismographic Station

Colorful Rock ▲

20430

Nahal Zihor

20430

▲ Mt. Amram

20431

Raham Water Holes ▲

▲ 648

▲ Puah Hill

Amram Hill ▲

▲ 475

Raham Palms ▲

20462

2043C

Amram Lookout Point ⚘

Amram Pillars ▲

20460

20440

Campground ■

297 ▲ Bahat Hill

Nahal Raham

20465

20452

20452

20453

20451

▲ 443
Mt. Amir

To Nahal Shehoret

To Nahal Shehoret

Route 36:
Grand Finale in the South

This strenuous hike takes you from the Shehoret Canyon in the Eilat Mountains, along the last 25 kilometers of the Israel Trail, to the Taba Mountains.

Route length: 25 km.
Difficulty: For good hikers.
Start point: Nahal Shehoret Campsite.
Access: Drive down blue-marked track (20440) that starts at kilometer marker 20 on Route 90. Turn left onto green track (20441) and drive to campsite at intersection with black track (20555).
End point: Taba Border Crossing.
Early Ending Points: Route 12 beside Mt. Yoash – after 11 km; Rehavam Hill – after 17 km; Eilat Field Study Center – 1.5 km less than the full route.
Duration: 11 hours.
Admission fees: None.
Opening hours: None.
Equipment: Regular.
Remarks: There is no water along the route, so make sure to bring your own.
Pickup point for cars: End of route.
Map: Eilat Mountains Hiking and Trail Map (No. 20, English edition).

jan | feb | mar | apr | may | jun | jul | aug | sep | oct | nov | dec

Start early, very early. In order to do this, camp out beside the canyon of Nahal Shehoret, the starting point for our long hike. Walk down the green-marked track which soon turns into a trail (20457) that unites with the Israel Trail. The walk up the riverbed along the Israel Trail is a pleasant way to begin. In the morning the canyon is lovely, with dark, beautiful rocks. Even the dry waterfall (approximately 4 meters high), where the winding channel narrows to a width of only 2 meters, isn't a particularly big challenge. All you need is a gentle push from the people behind you, and a helping hand for the last person in the group.

A Little Lesson in Geology

At the point where the riverbed meets the northern slope of Mt. Shehoret (586 meters above sea level), a steep, high wall rises before you. Mt. Shehoret is a large slanted mass, surrounded by a fault line. It is also the brightest place in the area, since the mountain consists mainly of limestone. The mountain was given its name, which derives from the Hebrew word *shahor* (black), because of the dark riverbed by the same name at its foot.

The Israel Trail climbs southward (left) following a red trail (20464) to a lower saddle, where limestone meets granite. This means that nearly every step bounces the hiker back and forth hundreds of millions of years. The top of the saddle affords a nice view, including colorful Mt. Amir in the north and Mt. Shlomo in the south.

Beyond the saddle, the multicolored sandstone comes into sight. The walk in Nahal Shehoret was along the solid base of Israel's geological history, rock that slowly solidified from liquid magma in the depths of the earth's crust. This base marks the northern edge of the Arabo-Nubian Massif, which formed more than 550 million years ago.

The sandstone, on the other hand, formed much later, in the Lower Cretaceous period (141 to 100 million years ago), when the area consisted of dry land. It stratified on the massif after it was carried by rivers that drained from Sinai, Jordan, and Saudi Arabia. The colors of the sandstone come from various oxides, whose origin is not completely clear. At the end of the Lower Cretaceous period, for about 70 million years, a sea flooded the area and the limestone formed in it, stratified onto the sandstone. Geological activity is still taking place in this area. Entire layers have been destroyed by erosion and others have been shifted by faults.

"Lost Gorge"

The trail leads through colored sandstone to the large valley formed by Nahal Roded. A very short black-marked trail makes a detour to the east (right) and enters a very short hidden crevice, which has acquired the picturesque name of "Lost Gorge." Blocks of sandstone in the crevice rise to a height of more than 20 meters, resembling the famous Solomon's Pillars. Some call them "the Roded Pillars."

The broad valley of Nahal Roded was formed by the river digging its way through a large geological fault line. It collects enough water to sustain the large Negev acacias (*Acacia gerrardii* in Latin, *shitat hanegev* in Hebrew) that grow in it. A few of these trees have unfortunately dried out and died, apparently because the acacia strap flower, a parasitical plant with reddish flowers hanging from the trees.

On the edge of the valley, on a slope descending from Mt. Yehoahaz, a large group of rock piles can be seen, with a blue-marked trail leading to them (20467). This is Horvat Roded – a site containing a group of small structures situated in artificial depressions. Archaeologist Dr. Ze'ev Meshel thinks the site was used as a quarry in the Byzantine period and not as a settlement, and the quarriers used the hewn sections to build small rooms for their living quarters.

The only problem with this theory is that there are no Byzantine buildings nearby, so it is not clear where the quarriers took the hewn stones. It may be that they found this site to be a good source of stone for building roofs and so they hauled the stone to the Byzantine town of Ayla (Eilat).

Nahal Netafim

The trail now reaches the watershed between Nahal Roded and Nahal Netafim, and turns black, descending into Nahal Netafim along a narrow riverbed, flanked by upright walls 10 meters high. The trail runs along the line between sandstone and granite, with its hue changing back and forth between pink and dark shades.

When the Israel Trail, together with a trail marked in green, meets Nahal Netafim, it turns right, up the riverbed. Continue walking in the riverbed, along the trail that is marked in black (20472), through a canyon that is about 700 meters long and features a series of little dry waterfalls with colorful intrusions in the walls of the canyon. Then retrace your steps back to the Israel Trail, which circumvents the canyon from the

right, along the trail marked in green (20469), and reaches Ein Netafim – a tiny spring whose water drips into a man-made trough at the rate of 15 liters per hour. Eventually, the water fills the trough, which is about 2 meters long and about 1 meter wide. Southern maidenhair ferns contribute a fresh green hue to this spring, which is an important source of water for the local wildlife.

After stopping at the spring, climb the ladder of handles implanted in the rock crevice and then follow the Israel Trail up the dirt road (20468) to the western border highway (Route 12). Here we turn left, toward Mt. Yoash (734 meters above sea level), which rises beside the road. Before the mountain, the Israel Trail makes a right turn on a narrow ridge separating Nahal Yoash and Nahal Gishron (blue trail, 20570).

Nahal Gishron

Once across the highway, the landscape changes. To our left are the sandstone cliffs of Nahal Yoash, one of the rivulets of Nahal Shlomo. A little bit further down are the wild landscapes of Nahal Gishron, a deep crevice between steep, dark mountains, descending from the Eilat Mountains toward Sinai. Nearly opposite, beyond the riverbed, border marker No. 87 can easily be seen.

The trail passes the large blocks of sandstone strewn around the slope of Nahal Gishron circumventing the canyon of the upper part of the riverbed, which is across the border. The trail runs through a narrow, steep groove with a rope attached to the wall to help on the climb down.

The groove widens to a narrow, pretty riverbed and leads to a dry waterfall,

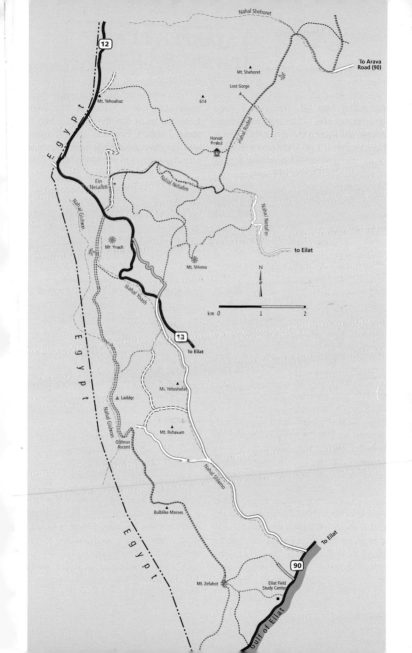

implanted with two 8-meter-high ladders — a rope ladder and an iron ladder. A bit further down the riverbed is another ladder. After taking advantage of these aids, continue along the trail to the foot of a reddish granite dry waterfall, 25 meters high, in the main channel of Nahal Gishron.

Further on, the riverbed digs its way through spectacular colored sandstone. On the left (north) you can make out blurred ancient rock carvings, depicting ibexes and groups of camel riders — perhaps a hunting scene.

Some 30 meters before the sign stating "Tzafra Pass," also to the left, are additional rock carvings. "Tzafra Pass," by the way, is named after a plump hiker who got stuck in the narrow crevice leading to Nahal Shlomo many years ago.

The riverbed of Nahal Gishron becomes narrower on its way down, creating little dry waterfalls, which are easily navigable until the Gishron Ascent, which climbs steeply up the left (northern) bank of the riverbed. Be careful not to continue walking down the riverbed — it leads into Egyptian territory.

The ascent ends at a very narrow ridge on whose other side is a white conical hill, which is completely different in character from the surrounding mountains. This is Rehavam Hill (not to be confused with the nearby Mt. Rehavam), situated in the heart of a syncline, in which sedimentary rocks were deposited in the Eocene epoch, when the ancient Tethys Ocean flooded the region and reached this point. Most of the syncline is covered with soft chalk, but at the top of Rehavam Hill there is still hard limestone, which has managed to preserve the soft

slopes below it. A good vehicular road (20563) leads to the ridge from Nahal Shlomo, so hikers can arrange to be picked up at this point if they wish to stop here.

Continue on the trail (20564, black), which reaches a large, impressive wall of smooth, stone and continues atop the wall. The black trail changes its color to red (20565), and later back to black, seemingly for no reason. But there is one, which has to do with the history of the trails in the area. In the past, the red trail led up from Tmilat Taba (*tmilat* is an Arabic word referring to a spot where water is buried under the surface of a dry riverbed) on an ascent that passed large bulblike limestone masses strewn on the ground. Since Tmilat Taba is situated in Sinai, people hiking the Israel Trail can only enjoy the bulblike masses at the top of the ascent, which is the meeting point of the red and black trails.

Smashing Conclusion

From the top of the ascent, the trail continues to the summit of Mt. Zefahot, which is only 278 meters above sea level but offers a marvelous view of the Gulf of Eilat and the Mountains of Edom.

From here follow the Israel Trail down toward the sea between mountains of schist (*zefahot*), granite, and an enormous variety of stunning metamorphic rocks. The Coral Island can be glimpsed from time to time in between the mountains.

The trail unites with a short dirt road and leads down to the highway, very close to the Eilat Princess Hotel. At the highway, a bit before Taba and the Israel-Egyptian border, the Israel Trail reaches its southernmost point.